Enjoy the story,

Jim
Duadulla

King of Clubs

King of Clubs

The Great Golf Marathon of 1938

JIM DUCIBELLA

Potomac Books
Washington, D.C.

Published in the United States by Potomac Books, Inc. All rights reserved. No part of this book may be reproduced in any manner whatsoever without written permission from the publisher, except in the case of brief quotations embodied in critical articles and reviews.

Library of Congress Cataloging-in-Publication Data
Ducibella, Jim.
  King of clubs : the great golf marathon of 1938 / Jim Ducibella. — 1st ed.
     p. cm.
  Includes bibliographical references.
  ISBN 978-1-59797-836-1 (hardcover)
  ISBN 978-1-59797-837-8 (electronic edition)
  1. Golf—United States—History—20th century. 2. Ferebee, J. Smith. 3. Tuerk, Fred. I. Title.
  GV981.D84 2012
  796.352097309043—dc23

                                                                2011042168

Printed in the United States of America on acid-free paper that meets the American National Standards Institute Z39-48 Standard.

Potomac Books
22841 Quicksilver Drive
Dulles, Virginia 20166

First Edition

10 9 8 7 6 5 4 3 2

For Mom and the Pestillos,
Dad and the Duces

Contents

1

Some Real Money

"Honestly, Smitty, you throw around the bullshit more diligently than any man I've ever known."

The well-heeled posse crowding James Smith "Smitty" Ferebee's locker at Olympia Fields Country Club whirled in unison to discover the source of this indelicate interruption.

Ferebee, who had been offering the details of how he had just finished playing 90 holes of golf—a story none of his fellow Chicagoans would have believed had it not involved Ferebee—reached for his tie and dropped it around his tanned, leathery neck. He didn't turn around with the others. He didn't have to.

Fred Tuerk had been his guest at the club the previous evening. The two stockbrokers were friends and rivals, each with offices at 120 South LaSalle Street in the heart of Chicago's financial district. Ferebee managed the Chicago branch of Barney Johnson and Company, while Tuerk was a partner in Fuller, Cruttenden and Company.

Drawn by the commotion at Ferebee's locker, Tuerk stood behind the crowd and waited for his friend to complete one of his typically self-serving tales. He yawned.

Lately, Tuerk had become increasingly bored by all of Ferebee's fanciful yarns. Their eight-year friendship, forged in 1930 amid the ornate octagonal columns of the Chicago Stock Exchange floor, was crumbling, a victim, amazingly enough, of unexpected good fortune. In the spring of 1937, Ferebee had convinced Tuerk that they should spend $30,000 for 296 acres of land on the shores of Linkhorn Bay and Broad Bay in Princess Anne County, Virginia, a short distance from the Virginia Beach oceanfront.

In agreeing to buy into the deal, Tuerk had relied on Ferebee's insight, for his friend knew the land well. It sat adjacent to what Ferebee referred to as Broad Bay

1

"Plantation," nearly 500 acres of fertile farmland anchored by the manor house where, in 1906, J. Smith Ferebee had been born. More practical Virginians would have described Broad Bay as a farm, but Ferebee glamorized the place by filling Tuerk's head with vivid descriptions of busy workers who labored under intense heat and humidity to tend to narrow rows of corn, spinach, and strawberries. He told of watching three-hundred-pound blocks of ice being hacked apart and layered over carrots before they were hauled to the nearby steamboat docks of Norfolk and shipped to Baltimore, Philadelphia, and New York. Ferebee waxed on endlessly about the beauty of Broad Bay, the placid cove that carried his family's name, and an unspoiled island on the other side of the water.

Fifteen months after the purchase, the two men received an unsolicited offer of $50,000. As wary as he was delighted, Tuerk finally decided to visit their investment. He shouldn't have been surprised by what he found, yet the reality was startling. As the heels of his shoes ground into a road constructed from crushed oyster shells and dust billowed upward and encrusted his glasses, Tuerk surveyed the swirl of wind-blown, barren dirt. Unlike the nearby plantation where Ferebee was born, there were no crops. There were no attendant workers. There was no procession to the docks of Norfolk; no anxious buyers waited for Virginia produce in Pennsylvania and beyond.

President Franklin Delano Roosevelt (FDR)'s strategy to pull the United States out of the nine-year Great Depression had begun to falter in 1937, a reversal that continued into 1938. After having reached pre-Depression levels, production and profits had plummeted once more. Unemployment had risen to nearly 20 percent. Tuerk stared silently at an investment that was going to require patient management from afar, with no guarantee of success. There was only one smart option, he concluded: sell. Business was business. Nearly doubling one's investment in little more than a year was unfathomably good business in this economic disaster; indeed, it was spectacularly better than anyone had a right to expect.

His partner's response, however, was a well-rehearsed, stubborn recitation of Ferebee family history.

Although Broad Bay Plantation and its manor house dated back to around 1640 and had nurtured generations of Ferebees since 1854, Enoch Dozier Ferebee suddenly uprooted his wife, Eva, and their three sons and sold the property on January 1, 1907, just months after Smith was born. His reasons were never made clear. Some people claimed that Enoch simply grew tired of farming and maintaining such a substantial tract of land. The other rumor was that Enoch's finances had been devastated when he was lured into investing in what turned out to be a bogus copper mine out west.

Whichever story was true, it was a fact that Smith's uncle, Norfolk banker M. C. Ferebee, purchased a small beachfront rooming house on 14th Street in Virginia Beach in 1907, renamed it The Ferebee, and placed Enoch and Eva in charge.

Enoch's family never completely recovered emotionally from the move. The stories Smitty's mother and older brothers recounted of Broad Bay Manor and the life they had enjoyed there mesmerized the youngster.

Now thirty-two years old and increasingly successful, Ferebee made no secret of his desire to return to Princess Anne County with his wife, Angeline (Angie), and to reclaim Broad Bay Plantation and the manor house. He'd never been given any indication that the present owners wanted to sell, but Ferebee's gambit was to maintain a presence nearby, just in case.

Almost daily in the months since fielding the unexpected offer, Tuerk had engaged his friend in a new, fruitless discussion. Each day, the tension between the two men grew. Ferebee knew it. When a business trip to Milwaukee was canceled at the last moment, he decided not to go home to Angeline. Without her knowledge, he invited Tuerk to Olympia Fields Country Club, a 692-acre sportsman's paradise on the outskirts of Chicago where many of the pillars of the community romped. He hoped that a guys' night out might patch the rift.

After dinner and a card game in the men's locker room, things between them seemed more like the old days. As daylight approached, Tuerk happily trudged toward one of the club's second-floor apartments. Meanwhile, Ferebee sought out Alex "Putter" Corrado, the club's caddie clerk, to see if he was available to play golf.

The most remarkable aspect of Ferebee's game was the breakneck speed with which he attacked the course. He preferred to think of his style as "purposeful." Either way, friends joked that he could play 18 holes in the time it took some of them to finish stretching. He'd long ago abandoned casual conversation on the course and had begun hurling himself through a round as if the happiest moment of his life would begin immediately after the next swing.

Corrado's job as the caddie clerk was to pay the club's young caddies. As a playing partner, he had two great assets: he was always on the premises at the crack of dawn, and he could keep pace with Ferebee.

With the sun beginning to rise and lush green fairways unpopulated for as far as the eye could see, Olympia Fields and its four majestic courses stood as close to perfection as Ferebee could imagine.

They finished Course Number 1 by 7 a.m. and Number 2 at 8:45. Inspired by the speed and skill with which they were playing, the duo was through with Number 3 by 11. Then it was on to the club's crown jewel, Course Number 4, site of the 1928 U.S. Open. After completing the round at 12:45 p.m., they proceeded back to Course Number 1 and played it again—90 holes in all—before the late-July heat and fairways jammed with slowpoke players finally drove them inside.

Ferebee practically skipped through the pro shop before turning left and waltzing down the short hallway that led to the men's locker room, whistling and waving at everyone. He'd never crammed so many holes into one day, and an adrenaline-powered afterglow coursed through him like electricity. Meanwhile, thanks to the chatty Corrado, the story was already spreading throughout the club that its most eccentric member had just completed a truly extraordinary feat.

Grabbing a cake of soap and a towel, Ferebee stripped off his clothes in the sky-blue-tiled cubicle adjacent to his stall and slipped into the steamy comfort of the shower. A moment later, a band of fellow members burst into the room, shouting his name as if searching the woods for a lost child.

"Is it true?" Adam J. Riffel bellowed impatiently, determined to be heard above the din of running water and flushing toilets.

Ferebee nudged the knob to the right, creating a fresh plume of steam. He lathered himself a second time, pausing to massage his tender feet. He rarely spent much time under a hot shower after golf, preferring a vigorous swim to soothe his muscles. But the rowdy intrusion by these impertinent "gentlemen" irked him so that he quickly determined that he would make them wait.

Riffel's voice, Ferebee thought, carried a trace of disappointment, as though he believed that he'd been deprived of a gambling opportunity. Since joining Olympia Fields, he and Riffel had played a great deal of golf together, primarily because Riffel could almost match Ferebee's speed.

They enjoyed an oddly competitive relationship. A frequent challenger for the club championship, Riffel was clearly the superior player, except when he and Ferebee had a wager. Then Ferebee frequently found a way to come out on top, after which Riffel would moan about how "unlucky" he'd been. While Ferebee bristled at the litany of excuses, he appreciated Riffel's unflagging commitment to paying off his losses.

Riffel also had unintentionally provided Ferebee with his most colorful of several nicknames. Several months earlier, the two had come to the 18th hole of Course Number 3, their match all square. Perhaps trying to rattle his opponent, Riffel bet Ferebee $100 that he wouldn't sink the 20-foot putt he was facing. Ferebee balked, after which Riffel sweetened the deal by offering 10–1 odds.

A moment later and $1,000 poorer, Riffel staggered past the club's signature cathedral-style clock tower and through the back door of the massive English Tudor clubhouse. As he entered the locker room, witnesses heard him muttering, "Fabulous putt, Ferebee, just goddamned fabulous."

Afterward, although most everyone at Olympia Fields continued to call him Smitty, those who knew the story dubbed him Fabulous Ferebee, or just Fabulous.

Folks did not always use it as a term of endearment. He was just so . . . different. Ferebee was lean and Hollywood handsome, with piercing blue eyes and thick, dark-blond hair. Even when serious, the corners of his mouth bordered on a smirk, the gateway to a personality that could be warm and caring yet often was curiously reserved.

"He was the most unique person I've ever met, and I think a lot of [the members] felt the same way," Art Caschetta remembered. Caschetta, who was seventeen years old when Ferebee joined the club, was Olympia Fields' Renaissance man: locker-room attendant, caddie extraordinaire, tournament organizer, even club maker. Although there was a fifteen-year gap in their ages, the two were often inseparable.

"All the other guys out there were big businessmen, set in their ways, even though in 1938 some of them were broke and faking it," Caschetta continued. "Ferebee tried to be different. He was a pusher. He didn't back off nothing."

Too often, his detractors claimed, those differences were coldly calculated to feed his insatiable ego. They cringed at his habit of entering a room jingling a pocketful of change. No one distributed money to the poor kids who worked at the club with as much fanfare as Ferebee. He never passed a youngster without reaching into his pocket and flipping him a nickel.

"Go buy yourself some ice cream," he'd say with loud cheer. While he never challenged the opinion of his critics that he was shallow, Ferebee often confided in friends that he was painfully aware the money would be put toward something basic, say a nine-cent loaf of bread. Olympia Fields, he knew, didn't sell much ice cream to its kid labor force.

Others used the sobriquet "Fabulous" with obvious respect. While even his admirers were convinced that Ferebee was a wack, no one could remember the last time he hadn't made good on a promise. Whether it was natural charisma or part of some grand design, Ferebee was at his best when he was the center of attention.

One day Ferebee and George Halas shared lunch downtown at the Chicago Athletic Association. Halas, owner and coach of the Chicago Bears, read aloud the newspaper account of a man who'd spent 15 minutes in the deep end of a pool with his hands and feet tied behind his back.

The more Halas read, the more Ferebee fumed. Not only would he stay in the water twice that long, he promised Halas, he'd even swim 10 full laps so shackled. Later that day, Halas and a couple of attendants stood at the edge of the pool and watched, mouths open and eyes bugged, as Ferebee plowed back and forth, back and forth, brushing the pool walls with the top of his head.

Ferebee was a marvel in the water. Earlier that summer, he had christened Olympia Fields' new 30-yard pool by swimming 202 laps. Sometime later, he emptied the wallets of a few foolish members who wagered he couldn't swim 1,000 laps.

"Rule 1: Never bet him," Halas would warn people when he introduced them to Ferebee, "even if he says the sun's not coming up tomorrow."

Now Tuerk was about to violate that dictum.

As some of the crowd around Ferebee's locker moved off, Tuerk inched closer and heard Ferebee talking about his scores. As usual, they'd been in the mid-80s. Ferebee joked that he'd never be club champion, unless the winner was the guy who played the most holes. The other golfers laughed. Tuerk rolled his eyes.

"I've thought about this for a while," Ferebee began, slowly pulling on his trousers in what Tuerk interpreted as an obvious effort at building suspense. "One of these days I'm going to play all four courses here twice in the same day. Hell, I would have done it today if some of the slowpokes around here had gotten out of my way."

That boast clinched it for Tuerk. It was time to call Ferebee's bluff. No one, Tuerk reasoned, could play 144 holes in one day, not even Ferebee. Tuerk reinforced that conviction loudly with a bit of profanity and a $100 bet.

"One hundred bucks? I guess you're not doing as well as you let on," Ferebee needled. "Put up some real money and we'll talk."

Tuerk was pretty sure he knew where Ferebee was steering the conversation—to their property in Virginia—and he happily went along. This impasse between them could be broken in his favor, but only by outwitting Ferebee.

The surprising detail about Tuerk's locker-room ambush was that he'd been able to slip in unnoticed. He stood 6 foot 3 inches tall, and his weight fluctuated wildly between 250 and 300 pounds. A good portion of that heft took up residence in his waist, causing every necktie he wore to come to an abrupt halt several inches above his navel.

"Fat Fred," as he was known around town, had minimal interest and even less ability in sports. Business and cooking were his meat and potatoes, with an occasional side order of women. He had played golf exactly once, years later telling his son that he'd quit after 16 holes and 173 maddening swipes at the ball.

Conversely, Ferebee was three inches shorter and weighed maybe 160 pounds. Strong as rebar, his only obvious physical imperfection was his calves. Despite all the exercise, they remained spaghetti thin and taut as a frozen clothesline.

Thinking on the fly, Tuerk negotiated firmly. "Before I put up another dime, we'll need some rules."

"Let's hear them."

Ferebee would walk every step of all 144 holes, Tuerk demanded, and every step between the holes. He also would have to tee the ball himself at the start of every hole.

"That sounds reasonable."

If he shot more than 95 for any 18-hole segment, the match would belong to Tuerk. Furthermore, once he started, Ferebee had to finish all 144 holes by midnight. Finally, there would be no rain checks.

Ferebee consented, but only if Art Caschetta caddied and they were accompanied by Charles Alexander.

Tuerk was only vaguely familiar with Alexander, a physician and Olympia Fields member from the nearby town of Harvey. He'd heard that the man was almost as eccentric as Ferebee was. He was a pilot who reveled in climbing aboard his single-engine Curtiss-Wright Travel Air then dive-bombing unsuspecting club members as they played golf, sending them hurtling face-first to the ground.

Despite such shenanigans, Alexander was revered at Olympia Fields. Frequently summoned to care for club members who'd taken ill, Alexander was known to whisk them from their hospital beds and move them into his own home, where he would nurse them back to health. A decade before his death, Olympia Fields founder Charles M. Beach placed a written request in the hands of family members that he was to be cremated and his ashes spread over the property that his vision had helped create. He instructed his family to beseech his close friend Alexander, and only Alexander, to do the job. After observing a proper period of mourning, Alexander chose the week before Christmas 1937 to carry the sack containing Beach's remains aloft and scatter them, beginning with the clubhouse, then moving to the golf courses.

Caught up in the moment, Tuerk could not have cared less that Ferebee was so insistent that Art Caschetta serve as his caddie. For all Fat Fred knew, the tall, lanky teen was nothing more than a set of broad shoulders. He woefully miscalculated the kid's value to Smitty.

After beginning his employment at Olympia Fields at the age of nine, Caschetta soon became the caddie of choice when most of the top amateur golfers in Chicago visited Olympia Fields. Too poor ever to have taken a lesson, Caschetta learned the fundamentals by observing the teaching pros at the club.

More important, Caschetta could quickly analyze a problem and pass on the solution in a way that was easy to understand. This ability made him invaluable to Ferebee, who was also self-taught after an introduction to the game that melded sheer luck and his own quirky personality.

While at the University of Virginia, he'd entered a raffle and won clubs, a bag, balls, shirts, and golf shoes. Immediately, he agreed to sell them to a classmate, who asked only that Ferebee store the goods until he returned from spring break. After staring at the equipment for a week, Ferebee succumbed to temptation. He took the putter and a couple of balls to a nearby course. The next day, he tried hitting short shots with a niblick, the era's equivalent of a 9 iron. The following day, he tried a different club. By the time his friend returned, Ferebee was rising at dawn to get in as many holes as possible before class, all memory of the sale forgotten.

While Ferebee's natural athleticism enabled him to shoot in the 90s, with an occasional round in the high 80s, he lapsed into enough bad habits to keep Caschetta busy. In the short time they'd worked together, the caddie had learned Ferebee's game, the shots he struck well, and the ones that gave him trouble. Ferebee had improved under the kid's tutelage.

Caschetta had played a major part in Ferebee winning his celebrated bet with Riffel. He had recently finished working a Catholic Youth Organization outing at the club and was walking past the 18th hole of Course Number 3 while Ferebee and Riffel finished negotiating.

"Art, come here and help me read this goddamned thing," Ferebee yelled over.

Caschetta told him that the 20-foot putt was straight but cautioned Ferebee to play a slight break because it ran downhill.

When the putt dropped, Ferebee leaped into the air and grabbed Caschetta as the shell-shocked Riffel trudged away. He invited Caschetta to join him in the clubhouse for a reward, but Art begged off, claiming that he had another job.

When Ferebee was out of sight and no one else was looking, Caschetta walked back to one of the holes bisected by Butterfield Creek. He reached under the wooden bridge that covered the creek and fished out a half-dozen plastic-wrapped packages of hot dogs and rolls from the clubhouse. He took them to his girlfriend Mary's house that night to help her parents feed their twelve children.

Tuerk, meanwhile, didn't see where the presence of either Caschetta or Alexander would put him at a disadvantage. "Then we'll play for the land," he proclaimed. "Winner takes all."

"You're on, Fred."

Witnesses to the bet had no idea what Tuerk and Ferebee were talking about, but it didn't stop them from jumping into the fray. By the time Ferebee finished combing his hair and straightening his tie, he had taken on another $2,500 in bets.

Tuerk wanted the matter settled the next day. Ferebee suddenly froze. He had never told his wife of his change in plans. For all Angeline knew, he was in Milwaukee.

After nine years of marriage, during which he had collected on a slew of crazy bets, or "hooey angles," as Angeline referred to them, Ferebee knew she would be adamantly opposed to risking the precious Virginia property over a triviality like golf.

No, he implored Tuerk, this bet must be handled discreetly. Angeline was starting a vacation in Virginia on August 4. He would see Tuerk at Olympia Fields on August 5.

2

A Ferebee Never Quits

Everything about Olympia Fields defined gargantuan. Located 26 miles south of Chicago, the club sat on land that had been home to more than 20 farms before being discovered by Charles M. Beach in the fall of 1913.

Beach was a transplanted New Englander whose background was shrouded in mystery. The only year he appeared in a Chicago phone directory was 1912, in which he was listed as a salesman. That description would have been news to the club's charter members. They had heard that he'd worked as a small-town school-teacher before switching to contracting and real estate.

None of those occupations left Beach flush with cash, and he distributed much of what he had to support underprivileged children. He spent the final 15 years of his life as a guest of the club he founded. When he died in 1937, his estate was negligible.

But what he lacked in money, he more than made up for in imagination and vision. In the pamphlet that passed for his memoir, he expressed disdain for Chicago's other country clubs, which offered "limited memberships" and re-stricted "facilities." His goal for Olympia Fields was to satisfy the "golf-hungry businessman."

Ultimately, it took more than the four championship courses to achieve that objective. In 1925, after years of contentious planning, he unveiled a clubhouse unlike any other in America. In a city that since World War I had prided itself on architecture that tickled the clouds, the clubhouse at Olympia Fields redefined breathtaking in a new, lateral, direction.

Beach and the club's first three presidents—among them legendary college football coach Amos Alonzo Stagg—worked tirelessly in planning the building. Then they brought in George C. Nimmons to handle the design. Nimmons had earned a rather substantial reputation designing commercial buildings, chiefly for

Sears, Roebuck and Company. But he also had designed Richard Sears's home in Grayslake, Illinois, and Sears president Julius Rosenwald's 20-room, prairie-style mansion.

Nimmons engaged in a liberal translation of English Tudor architecture, reminiscent of the best cathedral-like country homes from that period. His ultimate design imbued Olympia Fields members with an instant prestige by inspiring thoughts of English aristocracy.

Started in 1923 at a cost of $1.3 million, Nimmons's zigzagging two-story creation of precast stone and stucco roof would have measured 240 yards had it run in a straight line. The half-timbered, Tudor-style edifice consumed seven acres and included 79 residential apartments, barber and beauty shops, a "hospital" with a nurse on 24-hour call, small gymnasiums in the men's and women's locker room, its own ice-making plant, and dozens of basement workshops. Eventually, Olympia Fields opened its own laundry.

Thirty-five waitresses served Saturday and Sunday dinners. At the end of the weekend day, the staff washed 12,000 pieces of china, 1,000 glasses, and 5,000 pieces of silver. The kitchen churned out 4,000 meals a week.

The locker rooms were so preposterously cavernous that the same facilities from competing clubs Flossmoor, Calumet, and Idlewild could fit inside simultaneously. Road construction terms were used to describe the men's locker room.

A central thoroughfare led from the pro shop to a rear exit close to the finishing hole of famous Course Number 4. Intersecting the main passageway were "avenues" that formed the home bases for intraclub competition. It wasn't unusual for members whose tan, double-wide lockers were located on Gasoline Alley to pose a challenge to their neighbors in Tombstone Alley, Harmony Alley, Sally's Alley, or the Streets of Paris. Ferebee was assigned the last locker on the last row of lockers, known as Nu Alley.

Near the center of the 100,000-square foot clubhouse proudly stood the club's signature feature, an 80-foot, four-sided clock tower that immediately became the focal point of every photographer's lens. A spiral staircase, barely wide enough for a man's shoulders, curled up to a wooden platform fronted by the clock faces. It provided panoramic views of the four courses and the countryside beyond.

Wildlife flourished on the grounds. One member counted 74 different species of birds. Foxes, muskrats, weasels, and possums found shelter behind oak, ash, maple, juniper, elm, birch, basswood, and cherry trees.

In a final gesture of convenience for its members, Olympia Fields featured its own train station, serviced by up to 10 trains an hour from downtown on Sundays. It also opened its own post office, appropriately and ably staffed by a man named Stamper.

Until the start of World War II, members had access to swimming, tennis, riding, dancing, bridge, table tennis, a gun club, bowling (indoor and lawn), keno, skiing, tobogganing, polo, skating, trapshooting, and archery. The discriminating Chicago sportsmen might never have experienced anything like it. In the years preceding the Depression, membership at Olympia Fields surpassed 1,000.

But much had changed by 1938. Each month, the minutes of the board meetings contained references to members who couldn't keep up with their dues or other charges. Warnings were issued to pay up or risk expulsion. As often as not, it seemed, the latter tactic became necessary.

Each alley once had brimmed with three rows of 15 lockers apiece. As membership dwindled, Olympia Fields began selling off its surplus lockers to defray expenses. Not long after he and Angeline joined, membership had withered to a mere 590 people, the vast majority of whom wouldn't have known the first thing about Mr. and Mrs. J. S. Ferebee.

They'd never get past the basics with Angeline, more commonly known as Angie. She cherished her privacy and rarely trekked outside Chicago from the couple's home on North Mason Street. As for the man of the house, his most distinguishable trait in 1938 was that he would try anything and seemingly for any amount of money.

"I like to accomplish things people say I cannot accomplish," he often said. "It's more satisfying to achieve something when you prove the doubters wrong."

Until his bizarre wager with Fred Tuerk, few people were aware that Ferebee was a Virginian. His voice was as gravelly as Jimmy Durante's, but it carried no trace of Tidewater, no hint of tobacco. For all they knew, he could have hailed from St. Louis or Cincinnati. But the bet changed everything. Suddenly, members wanted to know more about the suave, impetuous daredevil in their midst.

One night after the bet was sealed, Ferebee held court inside the 73rd Hole, the club's nickname for the heavily paneled men's bar and grill just off the locker area. After a couple of drinks and a little coaxing from the curious, he finally shared his family's story.

The move from Broad Bay "Plantation" to The Ferebee, he told them, had done little to improve the family's finances. As he grew, Ferebee joined his brothers in performing many of the chores around the tiny hotel, including making the beds and helping clean the rooms. Eva Ferebee supplemented the family's income by taking in laundry and tutoring neighborhood children. His father, a beloved and congenial man with myriad interests, operated a general merchandise store for a while, but he abandoned that enterprise at about the same time he sold Broad Bay Plantation.

Smith grew up athletic and inquisitive, though he admitted that he was far less involved with books and formal education than his parents would have liked. Though occasionally moody, he had inherited his father's warm, engaging manner and his fascination with activities that required endurance, especially in the water.

It was not unusual for father and son to jump into the ocean and swim the 4½-mile distance from 14th Street to the Cape Henry Lighthouse, where the Chesapeake Bay met the Atlantic Ocean. After a brief rest on the beach, they'd plunge back in for the 4½-mile trek home.

When someone at the bar interrupted to ask why Ferebee took on so many crazy stunts, he told them of the day he and his father lingered a little longer than usual on the beach.

"You know, if you are in condition, there's only one real key to competing successfully in athletics," he recalled his father saying, "and that's mental discipline."

Smitty admitted that he didn't understand.

"You're a good, strong swimmer," his father continued. "You've got much more endurance than your brothers, and they're older. But even the fittest swimmer grows tired of the same stroke, over and over, mile after mile. What happens when you get tired in the water?"

"I told him that I wanted to quit," Smith remembered. "But he already knew that. He'd had to encourage me to keep going dozens of times. He explained that fatigue causes your brain to tell you to stop and rest, or that it's time to do something more interesting.

"My dad told me, 'Here's what you need to do: swim long enough for your brain to realize that your muscles are loose—then turn it off. Stop thinking about what you're doing and just let your body perform the way you have trained it.'"

Smith tapped on the bar to order a refill and waited long enough for those who desired to follow suit. Then he told them that he still had no idea what his father was driving at or why it suddenly seemed so important to him. But Enoch pressed on.

"'Anyone can learn this,' Enoch said. 'You're going to need it, because the best people you'll come up against in life will know it, too. And then, only one thing will separate you from them.

"'A Ferebee never quits.'"

Smitty laughed. "Judging from the number of times he repeated that over the next couple of years, I don't think my father was ever completely certain that I'd grasped the lesson. But it sunk in."

Young Ferebee developed a remarkable ability to ignore pain or fatigue, channeling his bountiful energy into outlandish achievement. As an adult, Ferebee didn't swim every day, but when he did, he might turn in 400 or 500 laps. He didn't play golf nearly as often as he would have liked, but when he did, 54 holes weren't out of the question.

On September 7, 1921, two days after Smith's 15th birthday, his father was summoned to the Norfolk sawmill where he had recently taken a second job as a supervisor. As he entered the wood yard, a saw broke loose from its control bearings and struck him in the head, killing him instantly. The grisly details were front-page news in the *Virginian-Pilot*, which noted that Enoch was a well-liked and respected man and a member of the Virginia Beach Town Council.

Enoch's death devastated a family all too familiar with unexpected, tragic loss. Smitty had been born two months prematurely and only three months after the death of his infant brother, Samuel. Another son, who was never named, followed Smitty but died during delivery.

While Eva struggled to raise her three surviving sons without their father, Smith enlisted the elements to pound away his grief. Day after day, winter or summer, he sliced through Atlantic waves from 14th Street to the lighthouse and back, seemingly oblivious to weather or water conditions.

He loved basketball. Although puny compared to the competition, he made himself into an indefatigable guard for a championship team at Oceana High School. On the wrestling mat, his unbending determination wore down opponents who were more talented but less committed. He won the respect of classmates, who elected him their senior class president.

He grew into a headstrong, mischievous young man with a comic touch. In high school, he once smuggled half a chocolate pie into a classroom and was about to begin eating when a teacher suddenly walked in. Panicked, Ferebee quickly slid the pie onto the seat of his desk and sat down.

His doting mother hoped that he would become the pastor of a little nearby church that she frequented. But as she saw the enormous pleasure he derived from his relentless work ethic and his utter contempt for convention, she reluctantly realized that his life would be considerably more worldly.

One area where Eva Ferebee would have her way was in Smith's choice of a college. Her youngest son would attend the Virginia Military Institute (VMI), and no amount of protest would dissuade her. Following his high school graduation in 1923, he headed for the hamlet of Lexington, with an unspoken intention to stay for two years before transferring to the much less stringent atmosphere of the University of Virginia.

Although VMI was located 240 miles from Virginia Beach, Eva's influence knew no boundary. Smith once complained in a letter home that he was bothered by a toothache. Eva immediately sent a telegram to Superintendent W. H. Cocke requesting that her son be allowed to take the train to Virginia Beach and consult with the family dentist.

Cocke replied, delicately reminding her that Lexington had its share of practicing dentists. He would gladly have an appointment arranged for Cadet Ferebee.

She offered her thanks in a return telegram but again requested a short leave for her son. Cocke assured her that an appointment had already been secured and that the problem was being handled.

She remained unsatisfied. "If it is a question of him missing class time," came her reply, "I assure you that he will make up what he missed."

Several exchanges later, a beaten-down Cocke finally granted Ferebee his furlough.

But there was nothing humorous about the letter Cocke mailed to Eva in 1925, late in her son's sophomore year. He was being dismissed from the corps for what Cocke described as the "brutal treatment of a new cadet . . . beating [him] on the chest until it was bruised."

It was one of VMI's time-honored traditions for upperclassmen to haze new students, called Rats, during their first year. But, in typical Ferebee fashion, he had carried it beyond what anyone could consider reasonable and had been caught. Now, something extraordinary would have to occur for him to continue his education at VMI.

Witnessing the depth of his mother's grief, Ferebee was suddenly imbued with a deep love for the school he had been so reluctant to attend. He mounted a frenzied letter campaign seeking reinstatement.

"Mine was the act of a fool," Ferebee wrote to Cocke. "But sir, let me tell you that even a fool can suffer if the penalty be disgrace to you and your mother—the only one that really matters. My suffering has been such that will warrant thought before act, but on my mother lies the telling mark.

"Can't you remember when you were a boy of eighteen, with a head harder than the hardest stone? Maybe yours was not the case, but such was mine. Warnings went unheeded; thought was a trouble to me.

"Sir, I say to you on my word as a former cadet that if you will give me just this chance you'll never regret it as long as the Institute stands and that will be forever."

Included in a mountain of correspondence he orchestrated was a letter from a Richmond post office inspector named W. J. Dixon. While on vacation in Virginia Beach in August 1925, Dixon witnessed Ferebee dash from the gift shop of the family hotel, jump fully clothed into the Atlantic, and save two men from drowning. When onlookers offered him a reward, he refused to accept it.

"In talking to him, I found that his one great ambition was to be restored to his old status at VMI," Dixon wrote. "This seems to be a deserving case. . . . He no doubt has in his make-up that which will reflect credit on a graduate of your school."

Dixon added that Ferebee had been so unfazed by his heroism that he hadn't even bothered to get the names or addresses of the men he had pulled ashore. And although Dixon had offered several times to appear before Cocke and testify on behalf of his young friend, Ferebee declined because he considered it too great an imposition.

Cocke's return letter addressed the fact that the rest of Ferebee's school record was noteworthy. However, hazing had become such a widespread problem at VMI that the Board of Visitors was more inclined to make an example of Ferebee than to reinstate him. That attitude never changed.

Humiliated, Ferebee finally took Cocke's advice and transferred to the University of Virginia, where he followed a line of studies parallel to those at VMI. He found time to compete on the wrestling and swim teams for two years and received a business degree. He then briefly attended law school in Charlottesville before losing interest in the summer of 1927 and moving to Chicago.

The 21-year-old arrived with nothing but nerve. Leaving Union Station, he began walking north when he spotted the Italian Village restaurant on Monroe.

Parked nearby, its Buffalo wire wheels glistening in the afternoon sun, was a new Cadillac. Dropping his suitcase, he hopped onto the car's running board, took out his handkerchief, and began buffing the hood when an angry man dashed his way and demanded an explanation.

"I'm looking for a meal," Ferebee answered calmly, extending his hand.

"The hell you are. Most likely, you want gin."

"Well, I wouldn't turn down a drink if you offered it," Ferebee teased before pointing to the restaurant. "I can prove to you that I really am hungry."

Walter Darfler, an investment banker with the brokerage firm of Halsey, Stuart and Company, was impressed by the young man's moxie. He led Ferebee up a staircase to the second floor and into a long, narrow room decorated in the earthen browns and greens of the Old Country. In a tiny alcove named Il Conventa, the two strangers pushed into pewlike seats and talked. Darfler watched Ferebee polish off a basket filled with bread and breadsticks, soup, salad, and spaghetti with tender meatballs the size of oranges. By the time they left, Darfler not only had offered Ferebee a job, but he'd also invited him to stay at his home until he could find an apartment.

Ferebee left Darfler's house each day with nothing in his pants pockets except 10 black-eyed peas that served as a peculiar sort of abacus. For each new client Ferebee made, he moved one pea from his left pocket to the right side. No workday ended until all 10 peas were reunited.

"By the time I was 23, I could write a check for $100,000," Ferebee told his enraptured friends at the bar. "And by the time I was 24, I owed $100,000. I admit it. I made too many foolish mistakes early on."

Ferebee outgrew Halsey, Stuart and Company after about a year and joined another brokerage house, Logan and Bryan. He arrived for his interview and was immediately captivated by the boss's secretary, a comely but shy 20-year-old named Angeline Puetz.

"I've never had a day like that, before or since," Ferebee enthused. "I got my dream job and my dream girl."

Ferebee concluded that that story was as much about him as anyone needed to know.

"The rest, as they say, is history," he told the barflies, insistent on maintaining his wife's privacy.

Angie was a second-generation Chicagoan whose forefathers had hurled themselves into the fabric of the city and their new country with a fury. Grandfather Theodore Puetz was born in Germany and came to Chicago bearing a saber scar on one cheek from his service in the Franco-Prussian War of 1870. On the night of the Great Fire in 1871, Puetz grabbed a bucket and dashed down to the river to assist firefighters. His real profession, as a gardener at the Garfield Park Conservatory, was much less harrowing.

Angie's father, Hubert, also ran off to war at a tender age. This time it was to Cuba for the Spanish-American War of 1898, after which the 18-year-old returned to Chicago and took work at the Fulton Street Wholesale Market as the chief engineer.

Angie grew up smart and studious. A high school graduate who never received the chance to attend college, her penchant for organization and accuracy led her to type the numbers she entered in her personal checkbook. In short, she had the ideal personality to manage an office, and her bosses at Logan and Bryan regarded her as invaluable.

Winning Angie's hand was not easy. Everyone at Logan and Bryan knew that she followed a strict policy of not dating coworkers. Ferebee was warned to stay away from her because any romantic pursuit was pointless. That advice was all he needed to hear. He immediately bet them that she would not turn down his offer of a date. Angie found the handsome newcomer with the blazing blue eyes intriguing, but when word of the wager reached her, she decided to play a practical joke on Ferebee and refuse his invitation.

His offer came and she rejected it. Afterward Angie assumed everything was settled and Ferebee had lost. When Ferebee asked her out a second time, she accepted, only to discover that the bet had covered her *ever* going out with him. Nearly two months to the day following the stock market crash of 1929, Smith and Angie were married in Chicago.

His wife was everything Ferebee was not. He could be wild and impetuous; she was cautious and analytical. He was demonstrative, penning his devotion to her in cards and letters. Although she could be loving and affectionate, she made that journey more slowly.

Ferebee, the epitome of health and vitality, loved people and craved attention. Angeline weathered health issues from an early age, none more frightening than when doctors performed surgery to remove her ovaries after an examination uncovered tumors. She was twenty-seven and had been married for only six years, but whatever hope the couple may have harbored for starting a family was over.

While she never really understood her husband's addiction to the spotlight, she revered him and tolerated it as long as it didn't infringe on their vows. She once told her husband that she trusted him to be away from her night after night, dining and drinking with friends, as long as he woke up in his own bed in the morning.

Thus began a decades-long routine in which Ferebee would meet friends and business associates for dinner. Midway through the meal, he'd excuse himself to phone home, after which he would flag down a waiter and place a to-go order for Angie.

Although he and Ferebee were nearly the same age, Tuerk's story was quite different. Ever the businessman, he needed just three years to finish the demanding curriculum offered at the University of Chicago. In the process, he employed several innovative ways to fund his education. During the day, he worked as a clerk in the post office. When the carnival came to town, Tuerk would make a deal with the food concessionaire to rent his tent when the show ended at night. He'd then stock it with his own food, some of which he himself had prepared, and sell it to the workers while they cleaned up after the crowds had left.

In graduate school at New York's Columbia University, he studied under securities and Wall Street legend Benjamin Graham while working nights as a statistician. Winning a position with the Guaranty Trust Company, Tuerk returned to Chicago in 1930 and joined the city's stock exchange.

"I remember once reading a biography of Benjamin Graham," Tuerk's son, George, said. "I told someone, 'My gosh, his life is exactly the same as my father's.'"

Tuerk heartily embraced Graham's major theories on investing and quickly established a few edicts of his own. He never bought until he was thoroughly conversant with a company and its product. He knew everything possible about the men who ran the companies in which he invested. He never invested in a company that didn't have a sound, mathematically supported chance to turn a profit. And he never, ever invested in anything solely on the advice of someone else.

Tuerk already enjoyed a glowing reputation as a savvy investor. The sole exception he had made was that land purchase in Virginia. His deep affection for

Ferebee had clouded his business sense. He should have known that his friend couldn't possibly endorse a rational and even-tempered strategy for the property.

This problematic union with Ferebee would hardly set a trend. Still, it was embarrassing to have exhibited such poor judgment. His only consolation was that now he had a way out. Tuerk told himself that he'd show Ferebee the cost of injecting emotion into business once his little golf stunt failed and he had to forfeit all that land in Virginia.

3

Quantity over Quality

With Angie out of the way on vacation, Ferebee planned to slip quietly into Olympia Fields and spend the night before the marathon in an upstairs apartment. After a physical at Dr. Charles Alexander's office that he passed with ease, Ferebee hopped aboard an Illinois Central Railroad train at the Harvey Station for the short jaunt to Olympia Fields. Little did he know that a sea of reporters from Chicago's numerous dailies and radio stations were waiting for him to arrive.

Flash-crazy photographers snapped his picture as though he were FDR appearing before Congress. Salesmen mingled with the news sharks like pilot fish, beseeching Ferebee to take to the course the next morning with their product in his hand or on his body.

At the head of the line was E. W. "Ed" Cochrane, sports editor of the *Chicago Evening American*. A dashing, popular columnist, Cochrane had luxurious, perfectly coiffed black hair and an always impeccable dress that moved his press box colleague Damon Runyon to compare him in print to a wealthy banker. Cochrane was a star in his own right.

At a time when Americans seemed as fixated on the men officiating their games as they were on those playing them, Cochrane ruled over college football contests involving many of the nation's top teams. He also moonlighted as an alternate referee for heavyweight title bouts between Jack Johnson and Jim Flynn in 1912 and the 1919 bloodbath in which Jack Dempsey floored Jess Willard seven times in the first round.

Cochrane was also among the 20 or so influential Chicago-area writers and editors who received courtesy memberships to Olympia Fields. Ferebee was undoubtedly aware of the practice, which made his hope that the marathon would be conducted without Angie's knowledge inexplicably naive.

Cochrane broke the story in an edition that hit the streets just a few hours before Ferebee arrived at Olympia Fields. His red-faced competitors were left with no choice but to play catch-up.

Normally, Ferebee's stunt would have warranted no more than a few paragraphs, and considering the protagonist's marquee good looks, a tiny photo might have been included. It was, after all, merely another in a growing list of marathons, making Ferebee a flagpole sitter or a Roller Derby jockey with a putter. While Chicagoans seemed captivated at the outset of these events, the big city possessed a disarmingly short attention span.

But Cochrane was smart enough to realize that two elements made this contest different from the others. The first was Ferebee himself. Country-club types didn't normally go in for this kind of wacky exercise. They preferred to see other people sweat.

The other factor was the timing. The Chicago Cubs were traveling from New York to Boston for what figured to be a ho-hum series with the Braves. The Cubs had begun August firmly rooted in third place in the National League, seven games behind the Pittsburgh Pirates. They'd just changed managers, the equivalent of waving a white flag on the season. Nothing hinted at the miracle pennant run that the new skipper, Gabby Hartnett, would engineer starting in September.

Meanwhile, the Chicago White Sox were once again an American League afterthought. They opened August trailing the mighty New York Yankees by twenty-two games and were backpedaling fast.

Cochrane needed to fill space and reel in readers. He decided to give the Ferebee story "legs," that is, better placement and a larger write-up than it deserved.

Pausing briefly on the station platform at the club's back gate, Ferebee slapped some backs, shook a few hands, and smiled often. But he also was unusually tight-lipped. More convinced than ever that the story of this madness would reach Angie and set off a matrimonial firestorm, he replied tersely to the few questions he bothered to answer.

Shielding his eyes with his right hand and resembling a shy Hollywood star, he finally made his way up an incline and into the clubhouse. There, he met up with Caschetta and the four caddies who would work the opening two rounds the next morning. The boys would spend the night in a dormitory located on the club's grounds so they wouldn't be late for Ferebee's 4:15 a.m. warm-up session. They hustled off to bed early. Not Ferebee.

He and friend Bill Williams dined together in the Amos Alonzo Stagg Room, named in honor of the club's first president and legendary college football coach. Ferebee sawed through a thick T-bone steak, drank iced tea, and enjoyed a wedge of cantaloupe for dessert.

At 10 p.m., he headed for bed and a night's sleep that wasn't to be. The combination of adrenaline and the media onslaught had unnerved him. Dr. Alexander had advised him to remain placid for the forty-eight hours leading up to the marathon, eat sensibly, and, above all else, rest. In theory, it was astute advice. However, a wide-eyed Ferebee soon wandered downstairs to the 73rd Hole, where Williams was presiding over one last card game before he drove east early the next morning.

Ferebee sat beside his friend and absentmindedly whiled away the hours preceding his scheduled 4 a.m. awakening.

"I kept asking, 'Smitty, shouldn't you be in bed?'" Williams recalled. "He just shrugged."

On just about any other day that August, the dark clouds that hovered low over Olympia Fields would have been cause for thanksgiving. A heat wave that had stumbled into Chicago from the southwest had overstayed its welcome. Even the club's extraordinary labyrinthine watering system hadn't prevented some holes from becoming concrete slabs of hardpan.

After a quick breakfast of orange juice, sweet rolls, and coffee served at the practice range, Ferebee and Caschetta ducked into the tunnel that crossed under the Illinois Central tracks. They came up through some trees and were greeted by the other caddies and a smattering of well-wishers at the murderous Course Number 4.

While each of Olympia Fields' courses was challenging, Number 4 was a par 70 featuring 6,490 yards of pure intimidation. It was one of the most demanding courses in America, and there was only one reason to launch the marathon from there, Ferebee told Steve Snider of United Press.

"There's no telling what will happen to my score once I get tired," he confessed. "We figured it'd be best to get at least one round here out of the way early."

Number 4 was designed by Willie Park, Jr., winner of the British Open in 1887 and 1889. By his own admission, it was the most diabolical of the 170 courses that carried his stamp in Europe, Canada, and the United States. Park surveyed the finished product at Olympia Fields, one of the last assignments of a life fully devoted to the game, and proclaimed, modestly, of course: "I have never seen a more natural setting for a championship course. I am satisfied now that your Number Four course is the equal of any golf course I have ever seen, and I know of none that is superior."

The United States Golf Association (USGA) agreed. It offered the 1928 U.S. Open to Olympia Fields and was rewarded with one of the most memorable championships in history when dapper Johnny Farrell made birdie on the final hole of a 36-hole playoff to outlast the game's iconic king, Bobby Jones.

Unveiled in 1923, two years before Park's death, the course opened with a substantial trio of holes measuring 510, 430, and 404 yards. Park's third hole was the first of several brilliant bits of design, requiring a drive over a large hill to a narrow fairway. In order to reach an elevated green rimmed by bunkers, one had to hit a long iron shot over serpentine Butterfield Creek, which bisected eight holes. Although the creek was picturesque, Prohibition-era members often complained that it reeked of bad gin that had seeped down from bootleggers' stills upstream.

Starting on the fourth hole, Park really tightened the screws. Landing areas off the tee narrowed. He strategically placed bunkers along fairways and greens where members' shots were most likely to land.

Park favored gargantuan, undulating greens measuring 1,000 or more square yards, some bordered by large oak trees. They generally sloped from back to front, inviting players to scurry the ball toward the hole, always with the risk of running off the back side.

Caschetta hauled Ferebee's clubs in a lightweight canvas golf bag specially designed for the occasion. He shoved a couple of extra balls into the pockets of his dark slacks, draped a white cotton towel around his neck, and yanked the brim of a black cap over his eyebrows.

"It's time," he informed Ferebee at precisely 5:05 a.m.

The two caddies assigned to track Ferebee's shots were already in place about 200 yards down the fairway. A fourth, ball and tee in hand, was ready to run with Ferebee and Caschetta, replacing divots, carrying food, and moving to the next tee while Smitty finished putting on the previous hole.

With a smooth, silky swing, Ferebee sent his opening shot about 220 yards down the center of the fairway. Loud, appreciative applause burst from the tiny gallery amid the *pop-pop-pop* of photographers' cameras, all of which faded quickly as Ferebee took off running.

By the time Ferebee reached the seventh hole, a par 4 of 400 yards, a variety of wayward shots had pushed his score to 5 over par. The seventh featured an elevated tee into a fairway that curved slightly to the left. Trying to play his tee shot over a fairway bunker on the left, Ferebee instead came up short and in the sand. His first attempt out never left the trap. His second attempt fluttered back into the fairway and left him with a mid-iron shot of 165 yards to one of Park's typically enormous putting arenas.

His fourth shot stopped just short of the green. A fumbled pitch rolled well past the flag, and he needed three putts to find the hole.

The disastrous quadruple-bogey 8 vaulted him to 9 over par. He was already in peril of exceeding 95 strokes and losing the bet.

The eighth hole, a par 3, measured nearly 200 yards, with three yawning bunkers to the left of the green. Ferebee managed to avoid the danger, but as his usually trusty putting stroke failed again, he made another bogey.

Ferebee reached the ninth tee and sighed. Wind that had blown at his back as he headed north off the first tee had switched, now coming at him as he traveled south toward Country Club Road. A 430-yard par 4 with fairway bunkers eager to claim his ball, the ninth was tough enough without any tricky gusts.

Under those conditions, Caschetta considered par to be out of the question, so he strategized the hole to play as a par 5: short tee shot down the middle, with the second shot deliberately shy of the green and the third onto the steepest putting surface on the course, below the hole, 25 feet away.

"Just lag it close," he advised Ferebee, acknowledging to himself the difficulty of that task on such a tricky green.

Ferebee tapped the ball and watched as it broke the direct opposite way he had envisioned. Fortunately, his 10-footer for bogey rimmed the cup before falling, giving Ferebee a 5 and an opening-nine tally of 46.

It was small consolation to Ferebee that he could play the back nine in the same score and not lose his bet. The wind was gaining steam, and he and Caschetta both knew more trouble lurked on the inward nine than it did on the trip out.

Nonetheless, Ferebee's putting stroke slowly returned, and his pars on the final three holes gave him a back-nine 44 and an 18-hole score of 90. Although five strokes fewer than he needed to stay in the bet with Tuerk, Ferebee's play was unspectacular except for its speed. He played the course in 90 minutes, or an average of a stroke per minute.

The plan from the beginning was to play 36 holes each on Courses 4 and 1—the two most challenging—then make two trips around Number 3, and finish with 36 holes over Number 2. Its layout was often referred to as the women's course for its relatively short and open design.

After uttering a few choice words under his breath, Ferebee headed back to the first tee of Number 4 while assuring reporters, "I can do better than that."

And he did. At 7:55 a.m., he tapped in for the par that gave him a score of 82. Then he headed through the back door to the locker room to change his clothes and shoes.

Fifteen minutes later, he slammed a drive down the first fairway of Course Number 1, opened in 1916 and crafted by Tom Bendelow, though his original work didn't last long. Park and architects William Watson, Harry Collis and Jack Daray—who also served as the club pro at Olympia Fields from 1924 to 1930—were brought in to tweak Bendelow's design early on.

A Scottish immigrant, Bendelow had worked as a typesetter for the *New York Herald* before making the curious career leap to golf course architecture. A strict adherent to the concept that the best course architects let nature do most of the work, Bendelow designed more than 600 courses, most with minimal intrusion. Included were the 18-hole course at East Lake Golf Club in Atlanta, where Bobby Jones cut his teeth, and Olympia Fields' crosstown rival, Medinah. As the director of golf for Van Cortlandt Park in New York, Bendelow also introduced the American public to reserved tee times, group lessons, caddie training, and course marshals.

Course Number 1 carried an unusually high par of 74 because Bendelow fashioned five par 5s and only a trio of par 3s. Butterfield Creek formed a natural water hazard on eleven holes. Nine holes were hemmed in by woods, causing Bendelow to offer back-nine holes measuring only 330, 255, 340, and 365 yards. But the course was uncommonly hilly, taxing a player's conditioning.

Ferebee, though, seemed unfazed. He needed only 45 minutes to play the front nine, though he was unsettled by an 8-over-par 45. Thirty-eight minutes later, he made a bogey 6 on the final hole, capping a comeback 37 and total of 82. More important, he stood an hour and 20 minutes ahead of schedule.

He had completed the front nine of his second trip around Course Number 1 in 40 shots, or 5 better than the first time. Then Dr. Alexander pulled him aside and handed him a cold can of Fox DeLuxe beer.

"A little change in diet never hurt anyone," joked Alexander, who decided that regularly scheduled bottles of beer offered the best way to keep Ferebee from becoming dehydrated.

By 11:06 a.m., Ferebee was through with Course Number 1 and halfway through the bet after another score of 82. He headed back to the clubhouse for another shower and new clothes.

The fifth and sixth rounds would be played on Course Number 3. A collaboration involving Bendelow and William Watson, another in a seemingly endless line of Scottish immigrants with sketchpads, the par-70 course of 6,418 yards might have been the prettiest of the four during its rather short lifetime. The course opened in June 1920, but redesign plans were already in motion as early as 1925. Why club members were so anxious for change was unclear. No one had ever matched or broken par. Six holes were wide open, affording a much-needed break from others that demanded an elusive combination of accuracy and distance.

The gallery waiting at the first tee had grown to several hundred people, most nervously watching an ever-darkening sky. Included were some of the leading sportswriters of the day, though Cochrane of the *Chicago Evening American* wasn't among them. Milt Woodward was reporting from the course while Cochrane and Jimmy Corcoran handled rewrites from the office.

Charles Bartlett, golf editor of the *Daily Tribune* and another honorary Olympia Fields member, was on hand, along with reporter Charles Leavelle. Near them stood Herb Graffis of the *Times* and Ashton Hunt of the *Chicago Herald and Examiner*. Then there was herculean James Kearns of *the Chicago Daily News*, the day's most industrious scribe. He would file 10,000 words, more than he had contributed earlier that summer on Ralph Guldahl's stunning runaway victory at the U.S. Open at Cherry Hills Country Club in Colorado. Earl Hilligan of the Associated Press and Steve Snider of the United Press churned out updates that their editors downtown dutifully dispensed across America.

Meanwhile, switchboard operators at every Chicago paper were pleading for reinforcements to handle the deluge of phone calls. Ann Garrow, chief switchboard operator at the *Daily Tribune*, later estimated that at least 7,000 Ferebee-related calls were answered between eight o'clock in the morning and eight-thirty that night. By noon, the paper had brought in nine operators, the same number it assigned to World Series games.

At exactly noon, with Ferebee in the middle of the eighth fairway, the heavens finally burst, though not enough to keep him from playing. Twenty-five minutes and two rainy holes later, however, the golfer and his caddies briefly took cover. Smitty pulled on a pair of spiked rubbers over his shoes before continuing.

Throughout the day, a never-identified broadcaster kept a running commentary on the proceedings. To say that his knowledge of golf was lacking would be an understatement. On the 17th hole, Ferebee skulled a shot into Butterfield Creek, but the ball caromed off a rock and flew onto the fairway. As the gallery cheered good-naturedly, Ferebee flashed a sheepish grin at his good fortune. The announcer, meanwhile, screamed into his microphone that he'd just witnessed what must have been one of the greatest shots in golf history and that only someone of enormous skill and self-confidence would have attempted such a nervy shot.

Ferebee finished round 5 by holing a six-foot par putt for a total of 87. His feet were aching, and he changed shoes and socks earlier than planned before returning to the first tee for round 6 at 1:40 p.m.

Fourteen minutes later, a new storm—more like a squall—blew through Olympia Fields. When heavy winds and torrential rain convinced Olympia Fields officials to send a car onto the course, Ferebee was halfway through the fifth hole. It transported Ferebee's drenched party to the safety of the clubhouse.

"I can't beat storms like that," Ferebee wearily told the AP's Hilligan while he stared out a locker-room window and watched wall after wall of water roll through.

It would be an hour and 10 minutes before it was safe enough to continue play. Almost all of Ferebee's hard-earned advantage against the clock was lost. Meanwhile, the friction of Ferebee's wet shoe leather rubbing against his white wool sock and bony flesh had created a nasty blister that festered with each step.

When Ferebee looked at Dr. Charles Alexander for advice, Alexander merely shrugged. The only immediate solution was to stop the friction, which meant getting out of his shoes and walking barefoot. That option was hardly practical.

Ferebee finally returned to the course at 3:55 p.m., 50 holes shy of winning the bet, and with a new plan of attack. Caschetta would continue to carry Ferebee's bag, and two forecaddies would continue tracking his shots. Two new boys, wielding bamboo poles, would sweep as much water as possible from the fairway area where Ferebee's shots were likely to land, and they would head to the green to do the same thing. Another caddie was pressed into service to carry Ferebee's sodden shoes over his shoulder in hopes they'd dry out quickly enough to be reused.

The strategy was only marginally successful. The water was everywhere and would not be tamed. Instead of putting, Ferebee began skimming the ball across the green using a 5 iron. Instead of blasting out of sand traps, he was forced to skull his shots out using his putter.

Nonetheless, he completed round 6 at 4:28 p.m. Then he made his way to the first tee of Course Number 2, unsure if the weather would allow him to finish the final 36 holes.

Watson designed Course Number 2 with speed in mind, carving it out of flat land with short distances separating one green from the next tee. Butterfield Creek intersected the course in four areas, and trees bordered fairways and greens on only 10 holes. Measuring slightly more than 6,300 yards, the course had a reputation as the easiest of the four layouts.

Except for a birdie 3 on the first hole, it wouldn't play that way for Ferebee, who by now was limping badly. One caddie, apparently unaware that Ferebee had to take each step alone, tried to put his arm around him to help remove some of the pressure from the affected foot. Caschetta yelled at the kid to get away.

Nonetheless, Ferebee finished round 7 at 16-over-par 88. He celebrated with another glass of Fox DeLuxe, while a caddie dumped powder over both of his feet and inside the two pairs of socks Alexander had recommended that Ferebee wear.

The rain had subsided, but the dark clouds remained low over the course, giving Olympia Fields a gloomier complexion than usual for 6:15 p.m. in early August. Waiting at the first tee was an exuberant, supportive crowd of friends, business associates, and club members that Hilligan estimated at more than 600 people. His back throbbing, his blistered foot raw, Ferebee pushed his peg and ball into the first tee one last time. The wind howled in his face.

After pumping another shot into the fairway, he turned and flashed a huge smile of relief at the gallery. "I'll make it now," he proclaimed confidently and started after the ball. The crowd followed.

By the time he reached the 495-yard 16th hole, Ferebee had exhausted 74 strokes and was struggling just to put one muddy foot in front of the other. Number 16 was shaped like a cucumber, or wide open off the tee before trees on both sides narrowed the fairway as one approached the green. Still into the wind, Ferebee needed four shots to reach the putting area and two putts to get in the hole for a bogey 6.

The 17th measured just 366 yards. Ferebee punched a 165-yard second shot onto the green to set up a par.

At 7:50 p.m., Ferebee stood on the tee of number 18, facing 420 yards of mostly open terrain with Butterfield Creek about 175 yards down the fairway. Ferebee cleared the creek by 20 yards and used two more mid-iron shots to arrive on the green.

It was 8:12 p.m. when his last putt hit the bottom of the cup. A score of photographers flashed pictures, and a crowd that had swelled to more than 1,000 people cheered wildly. Nearby, Fred Tuerk stood beside a bench, waiting. Ferebee plopped down, exhausted, his hair ratty and sticking out in all different directions. Tuerk, wearing a crisp black business suit, long-sleeved white shirt, and striped tie, gently covered his friend's right hand with his own and slipped him an IOU for his share of the Virginia property.

Stacked three deep, well-wishers watched the men exchange generous, sincere smiles before Tuerk retreated. Ferebee turned to the crowd.

"Well, my game has volume if not quality," he joked weakly.

Later that night, hundreds of miles from Chicago, Bill Williams, Ferebee's card-playing companion from the night before, flopped down in a diner, coffee and pie on his mind. A newspaper headline caught his eye:

BROKER WINNER OF 144-HOLE BET
FEREBEE TOURS EIGHT ROUNDS
IN SINGLE DAY

"On second thought," Williams yelled to the waitress, "lemme have a steak!"

4

Believe It or Not

Officially, Ferebee played 144 holes in 15 hours and 7 minutes. He struck 687 shots, an average of about 86 for every 18 holes. He walked an estimated 40 miles, or about the distance from Chicago to Waukegan.

Reporters for the *Virginian-Pilot* in Norfolk dutifully reported these statistics to a completely unaware Angeline Ferebee late that night after tracing her to an in-law's home near Virginia Beach. Whatever her initial reaction to what must have been shocking news, Angie played it off lightly.

"Gentlemen," she said demurely, "it's quite possible that my dear husband has gone insane."

Inside, as Ferebee intimated later, Angie was seething. She was incensed that Smitty had herded her out of town to Virginia without mentioning the bet. Such deceit was painful enough; his arrogance in not obtaining her consent made her wonder about the quality of their nine-year marriage.

On top of everything else, while playing 36 holes back at Olympia Fields less than 24 hours after the marathon, Ferebee admitted that in the strictest legal sense, he did not even own the land. And, he added childishly, as though two wrongs equaled a right, neither did Fred Tuerk. The only names on the title were those of Angeline Ferebee and Jean Tuerk, Fred's wife, who had been aware of the bet early on.

Following the marathon, Ferebee had showered, changed, and joined friends for a celebratory steak dinner before finally phoning Angie well after midnight. She asked how he was feeling, congratulated him on winning the bet, and listened as he stammered out a couple of feeble excuses and what he hoped would pass for an apology. When he finally paused, she quietly interjected that they would discuss the matter more fully face to face.

"There's a day of reckoning coming when she gets back to Chicago," Ferebee promised his bemused pals after hanging up the phone.

Meanwhile, the Chicago press couldn't have been more impressed by what it had witnessed. Earl Hilligan of the Associated Press wrote that Ferebee "did everything he said he could—and more. The plucky 160-pound Ferebee, who once wrestled for the University of Virginia, pinned a decision on time and the elements with a stick-to-itiveness that would not be denied."

Charles Bartlett of the *Chicago Daily Tribune* called it "one of the most amazing marathons for a strange stake the game has ever seen."

By the time Ferebee arrived at work on Monday, August 8, he immediately began sifting through what he estimated as about 450 telegrams. Ferebee removed his shoes, leaned back in his swivel chair, propped his argyle-clad feet atop an oak desk, and aimed a small fan at them. He shuffled through the correspondence in between congratulatory phone calls.

The majority of the telegrams parroted one sent by his friend and client Reuben Trane, the climate-control manufacturer. Himself a sportsman and avid golfer, Trane offered his heartfelt congratulations on the achievement of an "extraordinary task."

Other communiqués were prickly. The marathon was a fraud, some authors charged without explanation. From Portland, Oregon, to Pennsylvania, competitors challenged him to one-on-one duels to determine golf's real "king of clubs."

Three female correspondents, having neither seen nor heard about a Mrs. Ferebee, asked if he was married. If not, was he interested in being married?

Ferebee chuckled. The answer to their first question was yes, at least for the moment. Angie wasn't due back from Virginia for another few days.

But the most intriguing communiqué of all came from Doug Storer, producer for Robert Ripley's *Believe It or Not* radio program. Storer invited Ferebee to discuss the marathon and wager on that night's show. Ripley would be broadcasting from New York, but if Ferebee would make his way to the studios of WMAQ on the 19th floor of the Merchandise Building by about 8:30 p.m., someone would be there to take care of him.

Ripley was 20 years into a career-long obsession with the macabre. He had begun penning an illustrated collection of sports trivia for the *New York Globe* in 1918 before eventually focusing on eerie, unnatural facets of life, such as a boy who died of old age at seven years old, the hen that lived for 17 days after its head was cut off, and the man who survived after being shot nine times by a firing squad. During the 1930s, 80 million people in 33 countries read Ripley's cartoon daily.

In 1930, Ripley brought his peculiar world to radio. Fans and sponsors followed its journey across the dial with equal zeal, from the National Broadcasting Company (NBC) to the Columbia Broadcasting System (CBS) to the Mutual Broadcasting System. For 14 consecutive years, Ripley and comedy virtuoso Jack Benny battled for ratings supremacy.

The Ferebee segment would be the *Believe It or Not* program's second that night, following Ripley's interview with blind golfer Dr. William Oxenham. The show would air a brief dramatization of the marathon, then Ripley would introduce Ferebee.

The interview was a broadcast valentine, as Ripley ladled praise on Ferebee.

"Not in the memory of the oldest golfer has any [similar] endurance golf game been recorded, where the contestant adhered strictly to golf rules and shot a game within the remarkable score obtained by Mr. Ferebee," he gushed. "Unusual hazards existed, which made Mr. Ferebee's feat of dramatic and unusual moment."

Ferebee deflected some of the credit to Dr. Alexander, Art Caschetta, the other caddies, and Olympia Fields golf pro Chuck Tanis. He also graciously described Fred Tuerk as "one of the closest personal friends I have, and the gamest guy on LaSalle Street."

Hundreds of miles away, inside a three-room South Philadelphia saloon not much larger than the pantry of a Main Line mansion, the owner of the Sharp Stick pulled his stool closer to the Zenith Walton radio, transfixed by the conversation between Ripley and Ferebee. The Tall Man, as he was known, had abandoned his real name more than 30 years earlier, correctly supposing that surviving in a world of toughies would be exceedingly difficult for someone named Fidelus A. Notty.

However, The Tall Man was the most misleading nickname imaginable. Closing in on 50 years of age, with a meticulously waxed handlebar mustache still as black as coal, the slightly built Notty stood barely more than 5½ feet tall. A white apron scraping his kneecaps, he served his customers standing atop an overturned soda crate. The speculation was that The Tall Man was a reference to the sheer volume of the drinks he served. Anyone who watched him pour knew that Notty had no use for jiggers.

Equally intriguing was the origin of the Sharp Stick's name. Most people thought it was related to Notty's fondness for billiards, but he had coined the phrase out of respect for the few South Philly cops who could cuff suspects with a billy club without leaving behind bruises.

"Watch out for that one," The Tall Man would advise the prostitutes working his back alley. "He carries a sharp stick."

Most girls reciprocated by offering a monetary token of their appreciation. Depending on what he knew of their situation, he was apt to refuse, though always with the warning, "Don't let this get out."

It wasn't readily apparent, but The Tall Man had carved out a comfortable living. He also managed to put aside almost $8,000 during 30 years of scrimping and saving, pimping, and paying off cops.

The two sides enjoyed a simple understanding. The Sharp Stick featured a side entrance to a room usually reserved for cops only. Inside, The Tall Man set out a daily feast featuring cold beer and some of his best booze, fresh loaves of rye bread, and pickles the size of batons. Hanging above the table was a slab of the finest roast beef. For the longest time, the food and drink were regarded as reason enough for the law to overlook The Tall Man's small-time gambling operation or the room down the street where his favorite customers were sent for an hour of discount companionship.

Lately, however, they sensed that The Tall Man was abusing his privileges. The cops had been summoned to an increasing number of seedy hotels where still-disoriented men complained that they'd walked into the Sharp Stick for a couple of drinks and never remembered walking out, let alone with some floozy. Their pockets had been emptied, and garish red lipstick had been smeared across their chests in the shape of a bull's-eye.

On the night of the Ripley-Ferebee broadcast, the cops walked through the front door of the Sharp Stick and pulled The Tall Man aside. You and the girls have had enough fun, they warned. With self-righteous vigor, The Tall Man denied any involvement, pointing out that gambling, not drugs and women, was his passion.

"You know me better than that," he lied. Then he returned to his radio, where the program was wrapping up.

Ripley and Ferebee had never claimed that playing 144 holes in one day represented a record. Neither did any of the dozen or so reporters who had witnessed the feat firsthand. Those who covered golf regularly knew better. A few overly zealous copy editors had incorporated the catchy phrase "marathon king" into headlines, but those who were familiar with such foolishness scoffed at that description. They knew that using just four clubs, 21-year-old amateur Nick J. Morris had set the American marathon mark of 290 holes at San Antonio's Brackenridge Municipal Golf Course 15 years before Ferebee's stroll around Olympia Fields. Meanwhile, Morris trailed world record-holder Bruce Sutherland of Edinburgh, Scotland, by 14 holes.

But that wasn't how listeners and readers interpreted Ferebee's feat. Even before he answered Ripley's first fawning question, Ferebee's accomplishment already had been targeted by wannabe sports legends.

In Auburn, New York, 22-year-old Bill Coleman claimed he'd set a record after he played 171 holes in 15 hours at the Highland Golf Club. It turned out that all he received for his trouble was a 12-pound weight loss and a blistered left heel. That same day in Kansas City, 18-year-old caddie Charles Richardson logged 173 holes at the Stayton Meadows Golf Course. His feet badly blistered and his face severely sunburned, he was finally dragged off the course by his fellow caddies short of his goal of 180 holes. Despite winning just 10 bucks, he guessed he'd shown "that guy in Chicago" a thing or two.

While Coleman and Richardson tended to their wounds, Ferebee was making nice with Ripley on the radio. Hours after Ripley signed off on August 8, America woke up with a raging case of obsessive-compulsive lunacy.

On August 9, in Fayetteville, Pennsylvania, 22-year-old welder and part-time caddie Carlton "Lefty" Brown played 196 holes in 11 hours on the Caledonia Course at the Graeffenburg Inn. In jest, Tuerk clipped the story from the paper and sent it down the hall to Ferebee's office, scribbling across the top: "Looks like you're not so hot."

On August 14, in Richland Center, Wisconsin, 17-year-old Charles Herlitz played 153 holes in exactly 12 hours at the 2,500-yard Richland Center Country Club. Although the newspapers noted that the course featured only nine holes and played to a par of 34, one would have thought Herlitz had brought the brilliant Augusta National Golf Club to its knees.

"Without fanfare, the 17-year-old bettered J. Smith Ferebee's mark," crowed the *Oshkosh Northwestern*. The author noted that Herlitz's only concession to comfort was a 10-minute rest between rounds. If nothing else, the boy deserved credit for bleeding the most miles from an empty fuel tank; in 12 hours on the course, Herlitz had refused to eat.

Ferebee read a new note from Tuerk: "Seriously, Smitty, you're not so hot."

On August 16, in Bayside, New York, 26-year-old John Caruso, an accordion instructor who had been playing golf for only six months, breezed through 231 holes at a course unidentified by the reporting wire service. In claiming the record, Caruso played from 5:05 a.m. to 8:05 p.m., never exceeding 87 strokes.

Meanwhile, that same day in Portland, Oregon, Ed Labee and Joe Ahern played a mere 72 holes apiece, but they stretched themselves over two states and into Canada. The two go-getters began by playing 18 holes at the Peninsula Golf Club in Oregon before flying to Vancouver, British Columbia, for another 18. Then they hopped back to Seattle to play 18 holes in Rainier and another 18 in Tacoma before retreating to Portland. Amazingly, the two were tied heading into the final round in Tacoma, where Labee shot an even-par 72 to finish at 295, while Ahern slipped to a 5-over 77 and total of 300.

On August 19 in Newark, Ohio, 20-year-old Robert Anderson, a track star at Ohio University and the only contestant in a self-described "Bunion Derby," amassed 185 holes in 12 hours and 45 minutes at Moundbuilders Country Club.

The same day in Cuyahoga Falls, Ohio, two women, Sue Riley and L. M. Pieffer, combined to complete 180 holes at Breathnach Country Club.

On August 27, in New Rochelle, New York, Frank Carino whisked through 235 holes at Broadmoor Country Club in 14 hours and 30 minutes.

Two days later in New London, Wisconsin, 16-year-old Gordon Meiklejohn, a high school junior fueled by malted milks and chocolate, covered 237 holes at the 3,000-yard Springvale Golf Club in 15 hours and 45 minutes. Then his dad found out where he was. He yanked young Gordon off the course and sent him to bed, though not before feeding the teen a steak with "all the trimmings" and inviting a photographer into his home. Gordon's dog Whiskers provided the shooter with an ideal photo opportunity, slathering his master's face with congratulatory kisses.

The same day in the northern Chicago suburb of Northbrook, 20-year-old Joe Franco, nephew of Generalissimo Francisco Franco of Spain and a freshman on the Northwestern University golf team, turned in 301 holes at Techny Fields Golf Course. Franco hurtled himself from hole to hole while riding a motor scooter and being trailed by three caddies aboard similar transportation. Franco could do more than simply steer a scooter. He finished his exercise with a 2-under-par score of 1,204.

Tuerk's missives to Ferebee grew less lighthearted. "What's happening here?" he asked. "It looks as though anyone can do this."

On August 23 in West Chicago, six golfers played 144 holes apiece on the city's newest public course, par-72 St. Andrews. At 640 strokes, Joe Razily outlasted the others, averaging slightly more than 78 shots per 18.

Even the stars got into the act. On September 8, comedian Bob Hope "played" 180 holes in less than four hours at Lakeside Country Club in Burbank, California, a venue that Ferebee would soon come to know well. Afterward, Hope claimed marathon golf was a "snap, provided you use the Hope system," which was to play 10 balls at a time on each hole.

But it was a 150-pound housewife who finally plucked Tuerk's last nerve. On August 24, Josephine Baltrusis toured Chicago's Maywood course eight and a half times—totaling 154 holes—and never scored higher than 90.

The *Evening Tribune* of Marysville, Ohio, reported that the "golfathoner" did it "to show her husband she's a better golfer than he is."

"This is easier than housework," she said, and then volunteered that she would welcome a match against Ferebee.

"I won't challenge him," she concluded as she ran to her car for the drive home to fix dinner for her husband. "But I would like to see who can play the greatest number of holes."

While fresh marathon stories clicked in as quickly as the odometer turned on a speeding car, Ferebee was thunderstruck. For years, when he was asked how his little escapade could have triggered such a firestorm, he would quip that Roosevelt had gone on a fishing trip, leaving the nation to take out its frustrations elsewhere.

There was an element of truth in Ferebee's joke. Nearly 20 percent of Americans were without a job. Ignoring the advice of Treasury Secretary Hank Morgenthau, Roosevelt abandoned hope of balancing the national budget and instead launched a $5 billion program designed to give Americans more spending power. More money was pumped into the Work Progress Administration, Farm Security Administration, National Youth Administration, and the Civilian Conservation Corps. New slum clearance, housing, and highway construction programs were instituted. Credit restraints were eased. Congress passed the Fair Labor Standards Act, but the effects of a 25-cent-per-hour minimum wage and 44-hour maximum workweek were slow to be felt.

Americans scoured the bleak landscape, searching for outlets to help them forget their troubles. They continued to be mesmerized by dance marathons, where the raw misery of rubber-legged competitors temporarily salved their own considerable plight.

It wasn't long before only stunts that defied belief received recognition. In 1938, people were swallowing goldfish by the bucketful, so an Algerian immigrant to the United States warmed a plate of nuts and bolts with a blowtorch and ate them. Some enterprising, albeit twisted, souls even strapped water skis onto an elephant and towed him up the Hudson River.

Then there was Ferebee. In a year in which the average American earned less than $500, a $40 drop from the previous 12 months, this carefree, big-city stockbroker had nothing better to do than risk 296 acres of land and a couple of thousand dollars. While Great Plains residents coped with the final days of a three-year drought that had transformed their homes into a "dust bowl," in heartless Chicago this beer-swigging swan of a man flitted through the rain, leading a paddle of drakes who changed his shoes, carried his clubs, and powdered his feet.

Although some tried, Ferebee would not be goaded into action. Now that he had finished his fun and had his mug splashed all over the papers, he refused to meet the thinly veiled challenge of that pudgy housewife, that Baltrusis woman, whose performance the press lauded as nothing short of phenomenal.

"Mrs. Baltrusis has demonstrated that the recently much front-paged feat of J. Smith Ferebee . . . was not so much after all," read an editorial in the *Wisconsin State Journal*. "The feat emphasizes that even in the realm of athletics the male is no longer supreme. Women are proving that they not only have muscle but endurance and athletic judgment."

When Ferebee addressed the issue at a sports club luncheon in Madison, Wisconsin, one answer was all it took to shear off a large portion of whatever public admiration he had left. When asked why he wouldn't face Baltrusis, he replied peevishly, "I'm supposed to win, so it means nothing if I do. And if I don't win, I can never show my face on LaSalle Street again."

Tuerk read the story.

His final note came right to the point: "We need to talk."

5

A Trane Arrives

On the kind of tranquil late-summer evening that invites gentle conversation on the front porch, Reuben Trane bounded through the entrance to Olympia Fields and into the Amos Alonzo Stagg Room. He was in Chicago to celebrate his company's greatest technological success over dinner and drinks with Ferebee and a few of the stockbroker's friends.

The relationship between Trane and Ferebee had blossomed in the fall of 1936 when Trane hired Barney Johnson and Company to underwrite a public offering of $300,000 of preferred stock. Two years later, the inventor and businessman from small-town La Crosse, Wisconsin, and the big-time Chicago stockbroker often talked about how much they had in common.

In college, both had toiled in unappreciated sports: Ferebee wrestled and swam at Virginia, while Trane was a stalwart on the University of Wisconsin crew team. Now 52, Trane still maintained a ruggedly healthy physique, with only a single hint of his age. His full head of hair was a thick curtain of gray except for a dark stripe in the front that measured the approximate course of his bright, lively eyes.

An avid golfer who often competed in local La Crosse tournaments, Trane was at least as accomplished a player as Ferebee was. He was particularly proud of the hole in one he'd made on a 246-yard hole at La Crosse Country Club. It was the longest ace in city history.

The only son of Norwegian immigrants, Trane exuded the vigor, drive, and purpose of someone comfortable with leadership. In college, he was first vice president of his senior class. Later, he served as president of the La Crosse Chamber of Commerce. He was a frequent nominee in the local newspaper's Man of the Year contest and drew plaudits for giving "freely of his time and his money to any noteworthy cause that will benefit the city."

41

Summoned home to La Crosse after college to help run the tiny plumbing operation that his father opened in 1886, he had transformed the two-man Trane Company into a 1,500-employee force in the increasingly competitive arena of climate control. By 1936, air conditioners using Trane-manufactured parts were cooling the Wrigley Building in Chicago, the Astor and St. Regis Hotels in New York, Grauman's Chinese Theatre in Los Angeles, and dozens of other major office buildings and theaters.

Despite the public's sometimes indifferent response, theater operators and office and retail managers had valued air-conditioning as a business enhancer for more than a decade. Movie palaces, in particular, trumpeted the presence of air-conditioning. It was the vital component in their marketing scheme to lure patrons from their stifling and stuffy homes into a cool and comfortable environment where they could relax alongside hundreds of their neighbors.

However, lowering temperatures required solving myriad problems. Early air conditioners were dangerous, with ammonia, brine, or chemical refrigerant pumped directly into small units located throughout a building. Leaks were common and explosions always possible. Most systems required constant attention.

Thus, after much research, "central" air-conditioning was born. All the equipment was in one spot, and cooled air was distributed through ductwork. Yet it was outrageously expensive and required the sacrifice of valuable floor space for a bulky central unit. Installing ductwork in new construction was complicated; fitting it into older buildings was nearly impossible.

Trane and his engineers looked to a safe, inexpensive solution—water. Pipes could be run to isolated units as simply as they were run for conventional water supply systems. They occupied almost no space. The only drawback was the equipment that chilled the water. Burdened by a vast array of moving parts that seemed to give out at the most inopportune time, coolers remained cumbersome and expensive to install and maintain.

Midway through 1938, Trane and his engineers finally found the answer and developed the Turbovac. It still employed refrigerant, but the Freon was hermetically sealed within the unit and was used only to chill water that was circulated to the equipment. It was lightweight and did not vibrate, allowing it to be mounted safely on the roof of a building and freeing valuable space inside. With just two moving parts, breakdowns and repair costs would be minimal.

Even as Trane greeted Ferebee and Tuerk and was introduced to a Chicago advertising executive named Adolph O. Goodwin, his mind was sifting through ways to market his breakthrough product to architects, builders, and engineers. Long a believer in the power of the press, he was known to take out newspaper ads to congratulate companies on their purchase of Trane Company equipment. Nor was he afraid of less traditional marketing strategies. He had once used the grand opening of a department store to offer customers an inside look at how air-conditioning worked. One of his engineers conducted the demonstration, which Trane paid to have broadcast by a local radio station.

This time, neither of those advertising strategies appealed to Trane. The arrival of the Turbovac was huge, and it deserved a marketing plan equal in scope.

He pushed those thoughts aside as he and his dinner companions conversed about the most important topics of the day: the increasingly frightening shadow Adolf Hitler and the Nazis were casting over Europe, Roosevelt and the stall in America's recovery from the Depression, and the impact those events were having on business.

Normally quiet and introspective, Trane suddenly decided to lighten the mood by having some fun at Ferebee's expense. He joked about a recent editorial in the *Wisconsin State Journal*, which scolded Ferebee for not giving Mrs. Baltrusis the match it argued she richly deserved. Trane teased Ferebee that he must be living flush these days, for how else could he explain the recent news that he had rejected a Chicago newspaper's offer of $1,500 to play Baltrusis? He then told Tuerk and Goodwin about Ferebee's address to a group at the Stoddard Hotel in La Crosse, a short distance from Trane Company headquarters. The women, he relayed, were disappointed and the men disgusted when his friend announced that he had no intention of trying another marathon.

"People want to see you do something even more outlandish," Trane said, coming across more seriously than he had intended. "I understand why you're not interested, but you've gotten yourself into a real mess here, haven't you?"

Ferebee simply nodded.

Tuerk joined in, eager to pick the scab off an old wound. He explained to Trane and Goodwin that after reading about the many golfers who had outdone Ferebee's marathon, he felt cheated out of his portion of the Virginia land.

The normally unflappable Ferebee exploded. "Fred, you know damn well that I won that bet fair and square."

"Maybe."

"Maybe?" Ferebee repeated, his voice climbing an octave as it always did when he became riled. "What are you talking about?"

"Oh, you played all the holes and everything, but it wasn't as tough a deal as you made it out to be. People who aren't half the athlete you are—kids, for Christ's sake—have already beaten you, and it hasn't even been a month."

"You've got to be kidding," Ferebee replied loudly enough to draw disapproving glares from diners at nearby tables. "The housewife? Fred, you believe her story? I don't. The college kid on the scooter? You're not taking that stunt seriously! I don't care who did what. None of them played golf courses nearly as tough as Olympia Fields."

"That may be, but if it hadn't stormed, you would have finished this great 'feat' before supper," Tuerk retorted. "Hell, you could have spent most of the evening in the pool. The way I see it, that's not a 'marathon.' You owe me a chance to get my land back, and I'll bet you that these men agree."

"Let's get two things straight," Ferebee snapped. "One, it isn't your land. Not anymore. Two, I don't owe you a goddamned thing."

"That's what you say, but you seem to be the only person at this table who thinks this is over."

Trane and Goodwin exchanged glances, shocked but mesmerized by the sudden twist in the conversation. Ferebee lowered his fork and raised his glass. He rested the rim against his lower lip for a moment, then took a sip.

"All right, Fred," he finally said. "Sam Snead just took home a lot of money when he won a four-day tournament. I can't believe I'm saying this, but I'll play 144 holes a day for four straight days."

Now it was Trane's turn to bolt upright. "What!" he screeched, forgetting where he was. "Smitty, you're not serious?"

"Yes, sir, I am, and right here at Olympia Fields. One hundred forty-four holes a day for *four straight days*. That ought to keep everyone quiet. Right, Fred?"

Goodwin suddenly wagged his finger. "I'm not so sure," he interjected. "You've already played 144 holes at Olympia Fields. People will say you have a big advantage because you know this place so well."

Ferebee then suggested he could play 144 holes one day at Olympia Fields and the other rounds at three other local clubs.

"If you are really interested in seeing this craziness end," Goodwin argued quietly, "you should look beyond Chicago."

Ferebee raised his glass again. This time he leaned the rim against his forehead and stared through it at the rest of the room. "I have a four-day business trip scheduled for later this month," he said. "I'll pick a course in each city and do it then, playing 144 at each."

Suddenly, everyone at the table was pitching ideas that the group batted around and dissected. Trane wanted to know how Ferebee could make his appointments in one place, play golf, and still get to the next city in time to do it again. When Ferebee said he'd fly, Trane scoffed.

"You can't rely on commercial schedules; you'd have to have your own plane to even stand a chance," Trane told him, effectively ending any notion Ferebee had about mixing business into this emerging new bet.

Goodwin then multiplied 144 by four and concluded that 576 holes wasn't an exciting enough number. "Why not 150 a day?" he asked. "Make it an even 600 holes. And turn it into a marathon no one else would ever be crazy enough to try. Go from New York to Los Angeles. Believe me when I say that the press will eat each other alive going after this story."

Trane stared across the table in disbelief at his new acquaintance. Where had Ferebee found this guy? He'd never mentioned him before. If Tuerk's interaction with Goodwin was any indication, they were strangers, too.

How Ferebee and Goodwin came to know each other is pure conjecture. Caschetta, who was closer to Ferebee than just about anyone, said he'd never heard of Goodwin until just before the 600-hole marathon, and he never heard his name again once they returned to Chicago.

Born in Raleigh, North Carolina, Goodwin had attended Mars Hill Junior College before serving as an ensign in the navy during World War I. Most of his career had been spent as a copy editor for newspapers in Raleigh and at the *New York Herald Tribune* before he moved into advertising.

Ferebee glanced at Tuerk for a reaction.

"I personally don't see how this is possible," Tuerk said. "Just to be straight, if you don't do this, the property in Virginia reverts to me, correct?"

Ferebee nodded. "And if I make it?"

"I'll pay your mortgage," Tuerk responded, making an offer worth about $20,000.

"Deal," Ferebee said, extending his hand.

One week later, the men gathered inside Tuerk's LaSalle Street office to flesh out the details. The end of September—from the 18th onward—was open on everyone's calendar.

Trane was accompanied by Fred Pederson, his new head of advertising. Another native of La Crosse, Wisconsin, Pederson had been persuaded to leave Hollywood and return home earlier that year by his close friend James Trane, Reuben's son.

The two men entered the office armed with a plan. Trane had decided to rent one of American Airlines' newest planes, a Douglas DC-3 Skysleeper that would accommodate 14 people. The marathon would become his vehicle for introducing the Turbovac. Trane would conduct private meetings with engineers, architects, and builders in each city where Ferebee played. At the same time, he would market the Trane name to the public at rallies staged at airports or at the golf courses themselves. Trane assured Ferebee that he would foot the bill for everything, which he estimated at $22,000.

Ferebee readily agreed when Goodwin proposed that he take on an extended challenge, in part to give his benefactor a maximum amount of exposure. Instead of playing 150 holes in four cities, why not play at least 72 holes in eight destinations? He rattled off an itinerary: New York, Philadelphia, Milwaukee, Chicago, Kansas City, St. Louis, Phoenix, and Los Angeles. The extra holes needed to reach 600 could be folded in at several of the stops, depending on weather.

He admitted that he had already made contacts at the courses located near the airports in each place, pending the determination of an official date. If Ferebee consented, Goodwin would advance the trip, traveling ahead of the party to make sure everything was in order upon its arrival.

Goodwin also revealed that he had recently returned from New York and a meeting with officials of the 1939 World's Fair. Regaling them with the "inside" story of Ferebee's 144-hole marathon, Goodwin convinced them that his new golf adventure would be an ideal way to promote the fair. Ferebee was a natural-born showman, he assured them, who would draw for them an invaluable amount of publicity in some of the nation's biggest cities.

It wasn't a tough sell. Fair officials had read the stories of Ferebee's earlier exploit. But they weren't just going to roll over for Goodwin. They demanded that Ferebee finish in New York rather than start there. Also, they didn't want the marathon to end on a golf course; rather, they proposed that Ferebee play a 601st "hole" in front of the fair's Administration Building. That stunt would enable the organizers' invited guests to see the progress the officials had made on the fair grounds.

Goodwin said he didn't think Ferebee would object to any of it, especially if they would ante up a stipend of, say, $1,000.

Later, to make certain that Goodwin's assessment of Ferebee could be trusted, World's Fair officials conducted a background check. J. A. "Jack" Reilly, director of special events for the fair, sent telegrams to *Chicago Evening American* writers Ed Cochrane and Bill Margolis asking if Ferebee was "on the level."

Cochrane replied: "Golfer Ferebee is okey [*sic*]. He will make good on anything he agrees to do."

Margolis added, "Ferebee a high class LaSalle Street broker. Very much on the square. Very colorful and will do anything he says he will."

Back in Tuerk's office, after Goodwin relayed the New York story to an increasingly wide-eyed Ferebee, he quickly agreed. The dates of September 25–28 were locked in.

Pederson, whose script *Who Killed Gail Preston? (Murder in Swingtime)* had been made into a 1938 movie by Columbia Pictures that starred Rita Hayworth, Don Terry, Robert Paige, and Wyn Cahoon, was added to the retinue. He would handle the day-of dealings with the press in each city.

After catching wind that a new bet was in the works, Dr. Charles Alexander phoned Ferebee. Hearing the details, he wholeheartedly endorsed Goodwin's suggestion to include Los Angeles on the itinerary. Alexander tantalized the broker by telling him that he had a close friend in California who could get them into the exclusive Lakeside Golf Club, a mere 3½ miles from Hollywood.

But Alexander wouldn't name his contact, and he wouldn't call to arrange the matter unless he was included in the travel party. Ferebee gladly extended the invitation.

Again, Tuerk imposed a scoring limit, which he increased to 100 strokes per 18 holes because Ferebee would never have seen most of the courses on which he'd be playing. He was required to play at least 72 holes in each city and at least 144 holes each day.

As with the first bet, Ferebee would walk every step, with one foot touching the ground at all times. He wasn't to be lifted or carried anywhere. He had to tee the ball himself at the start of each hole and pick it out of the cup when he was done.

Ferebee had a few demands of his own. He wanted Caschetta to caddie for him. If the weather turned bad, he wanted the right to postpone play until it improved, even if that meant waiting until the next day.

They shook hands again, cementing the $20,000 wager and sparking a flurry of other bets. Trane and Tuerk threw in another $30,000 apiece, including $20,000 on whether Ferebee could play at least 144 holes daily. They bet $7,500 on whether he would play at least 72 holes in every city and another $2,500 on whether he would stay under 100 strokes for every 18 holes.

Barney Johnson phoned in from his office in Wisconsin and wound up betting $1,500 with Tuerk on whether Ferebee would finish the marathon. After the rotund Tuerk bragged that he would walk step for step with Ferebee over 600 holes, Johnson's hysterical laughter set the stage for another $500 outlay.

They all agreed to take a few days to finalize the itinerary before letting their old friends at the *Chicago Evening American* break the news. On September 14, the lead story in the sports pages belonged to Jimmy Corcoran, who revealed some of the details of what he called "the most amazing golfing marathon in history." A banner headline shrieked, "FEREBEE TO GOLF U.S.!"

"This one will be so goofy," Ferebee promised in print, "that I hope it ends them all."

Corcoran was back with another story the next day. It wasn't front-page news, but it was accompanied by a photo of the impeccably dressed Ferebee and Reuben Trane striding across a golf course, with Trane lugging his friend's bag. Corcoran detailed the apparent flood of wagering engaged in by wealthy businessmen on LaSalle Street.

"Several thousands of dollars have already been bet on the success—or failure—of the venture," he wrote. "Yes, there's still money on LaSalle Street when a broker sees a sporting chance for his chips."

Corcoran revealed that one man had laid down $10,000 during his lunch hour "that young Ferebee would make the grade" and had wrangled 2–1 odds. Word on the street was that other similar transactions had been arranged. It wasn't long before the press was reporting that $100,000 was on the line.

None of Chicago's newspapermen identified any of the bettors other than Ferebee, Tuerk, Trane, and Barney Johnson. That secret rankled writers such as

Herb Graffis of the *Chicago Daily Tribune*, ironically one of the media members who enjoyed free membership and free access at Olympia Fields.

"Mysterious are the details of the '$100,000 bet,'" he fumed in a column. "Who's betting the hundred blankets? Where? Why? . . . Maybe it's merely 100,000 yards of press-agent's salami that's being wagered. A few inches of salami regales; 100,000 yards of it regurgitates."

How much was actually wagered by and with the professionals in Chicago is unknown, and for good reason. On August 17, 1938, State's Attorney Thomas J. Courtney of Illinois had unleashed an all-out assault on the city's flourishing illegal gambling industry. Wielding axes and sledgehammers, Courtney's men had beaten or chopped down the doors to suspected "service stations." Inside, they had discovered hundreds of bettors, sometimes more. Countless numbers of bookies were arrested and led away, the furniture inside their parlors carved into kindling and their intricate telephone systems smashed into tiny pieces.

Day after day, the papers carried the details of successful raids by Courtney's "Battalion of Death." Several of the busts took place near LaSalle Street; one happened only two blocks from Ferebee's office. Some of the bigger bookies, knowing they were major targets, temporarily suspended their operations until things cooled down. Other shops went underground, moving to locations that had never been used before. Some bookies closed their doors but accepted bets delivered by courier.

In addition to Courtney's sudden crusade, an archaic legal rattrap known as Paragraph 330 of the Illinois Criminal Code had resurfaced that month. It had opened the door to a peculiar court case that had flabbergasted bookmakers.

In 1817, Illinois law set forth that any person who lost $10 or more gambling could sue the winner and recover his money. Moreover, if the loser did not bring suit within six months, "any person" could sue the winner for three times the amount that was lost. Half of that money would go to the local government.

Enter Mrs. Libbie Maxwell. She sued William "Big Bill" Johnson and four of his associates who were heads of the syndicate that Courtney conceded was "the most powerful and resourceful" in the city. Maxwell sought $45,000, or three times the amount she claimed her son-in-law lost in seven months of tough luck at Johnson's D&D Club, Horseshoe Club, Harlem Stables, and Devlin Club. Smart-alecky Chicago lawyers quickly went on the record to say that were they betting men, their money would be on the plucky Mrs. Maxwell walking away with the cash.

Apparently, the syndicate was too resourceful for Mrs. Maxwell and the state. There is no record of the case ever going to court. At the time, however, Ferebee and his cronies had no idea what the outcome would be, so they opted for caution and secrecy.

(One curious technicality about these suits hinged on their location. The year before, Miss Frances Moore's $150,000 case against one John Thermos was lost when Thermos's lawyer proved that his bet had taken place outside the borders of Illinois.)

Meanwhile, the travel party had to be finalized. Ferebee went to Caschetta's home to discuss the trip with Art's parents. Their 18-year-old son had never been out of Chicago before, had never been on a plane, and had never spent a night in a hotel. Ferebee assured them that he would personally see to Art's safety and welfare.

They raised one other matter. Olympia Fields didn't pay caddies who skipped work.

Ferebee raised his hand. "Of course I'm going to pay him," he said, as though it was a formality that had slipped his mind. "I'll give you 100 dollars right now if you'll let him go with me. He isn't going to make that much at the club."

The other details fell quickly into place. A friend of Ferebee's, Kenneth Beall, was named official scorer. Beall's brother, Jack, an Olympia Fields member, was allowed to tag along.

Fred Pederson suggested that Trane, Ferebee, Caschetta, Dr. Alexander, and, if he desired, Tuerk arrive in California on September 18, one week before play would begin at the posh and cloistered Lakeside Golf Club in Burbank. In addition to allowing Ferebee time to play a couple of practice rounds, Pederson assured them that he planned for Trane and Ferebee to make several promotional appearances.

The Chicago papers continued to hype the event. The balcony of the Stock Exchange trading room became the place for LaSalle Street brokers to meet and quietly negotiate additional wagers. Officials in each of the cities on Ferebee's schedule, meanwhile, were busy planning lavish welcomes.

At the Sharp Stick bar in South Philadelphia, The Tall Man filled his beer mug and was flipping through one of the local sports pages when a headline caught his eye:

"MARATHON GOLFER LOOSE AGAIN."

The story contained only the bare essentials, but it did include the fact that Ferebee would play 72 holes somewhere in Philadelphia.

The Tall Man picked up the phone, dialed Chicago, and heard a familiar voice. "So you know this Ferebee guy?"

"Yeah, crazy, fun SOB."

"What's happening with the books?"

"Four to one."

"Not bad. And?"

"I don't see them paying off—all that walking, flying, the rest of that shit. I love the guy, but he's lost his mind. Hell, he's not that good a golfer."

By the time The Tall Man hung up, he was certain there was money to be made off of Ferebee. The question was how. Carrying his beer into the side room to fix a sandwich, he devised an elaborate scheme.

That night, The Tall Man pulled aside a dozen of his regulars and proposed they have a little fun with this Ferebee business. He'd give them 4–1 odds that Ferebee would fail, but to participate, they'd each have to post $200 up front, no exceptions. As with the marathon itself, the wager would be broken into four parts, or $50 a day. The odds on Ferebee's first day of play were 2–1. The second day, the odds would grow to 3–1. The third day, they'd be 5–1, and the odds against Ferebee on the final day would be 6–1.

They could pull out only after the second and third day of play. But they would pay a $25 buyout after the second day, reducing their winnings to $25. If they pulled out after the third day, the buyout would be $200, reducing their profit to only $100.

When someone protested the high buyout fees, The Tall Man quickly replied that the bettor who stayed in all four days—and won—would walk away with $800. "Find someone else around here giving 4-to-1 odds," he snapped. "I'll save you the trouble; there isn't anyone."

The Tall Man couldn't name five people in South Philly capable of putting up $200 by themselves. But he knew the spirit of the city's most unique neighborhood, where Italians, Jews, Irish, and blacks worked side by side in the markets and the warehouses. Those who were interested in pursuing his challenge would go apartment to apartment, hovel to hovel, family to family, worker to worker, dock to dock. They'd collect a little bit here and a little more there until they had the money.

It wasn't long before he convinced himself that this wager wasn't so much a business deal as a public service to this struggling community. He was offering them a chance to make more money in four days than some had seen in the last four months. From the moment he unveiled his plan, he sensed the excitement on the streets, as neighbors scurried to form syndicates.

Only at 1110 North Mason Street, Smitty and Angie's home address, was there a noticeable lack of enthusiasm for the upcoming marathon. When Angie had returned from Virginia in August, she'd demanded that Ferebee promise he would never jeopardize losing that piece of property again. He'd quickly agreed.

Less than a month later, he had reneged. Again, he hadn't consulted her. She had not been invited to join the travel party, and Angie knew that her husband's decision had nothing to do with superstitions about women, ships, and bad luck. After all, she'd learned that a stewardess would be on board Trane's airplane, a radiant, young Texan named Lillian Fette.

When Ferebee arrived home on September 15 to pack for the train trip to Los Angeles that he and the others would begin that night, Angie wasn't there. On a table inside the front door sat a pale blue envelope, with a neatly folded sheet of stationary tucked inside.

Ferebee laid his newspaper on top of it and walked into the bedroom to gather his things. While waiting for the cab that would take him to Union Station, he peeked at the note.

"So much for promises," it said.

6

Shooting Stars

The *City of Los Angeles,* train travel's most elegant ride, pulled into the Union Pacific depot shortly after breakfast on Saturday, September 17. Dressed in sleek, dark business suits as though they were headed for work, Ferebee, Tuerk, Trane, and the rest of the entourage were greeted by Adolph Goodwin, reporter Maxwell Stiles of the *Los Angeles Examiner*, a photographer, and a surprise member of the Hollywood elite.

Gene Autry, known as the Singing Cowboy, was a longtime friend and occasional musical sidekick of Dr. Charles Alexander's. Ferebee's physician was also a guitar player and at one point had assembled a band featuring a piano player, bow fiddler, violinist, banjo player, and his first wife, the group's lead singer. Alexander had introduced Autry to some of his friends who were in management at the Chicago radio station WLS. The hit program *National Barn Dance* originated from WLS studios, and Autry soon became a beloved regular.

After Autry moved to California in 1935 to begin his career in movies, Dr. Alexander occasionally brought his family to visit. In later years, Autry would hoist Alexander's daughter, Madelyn, onto his horse Champion's back for a ride through the California countryside.

Once Ferebee's plans were set, Alexander had contacted Autry, who had recently completed filming *Rhythm of the Saddle*. He responded that he would have plenty of time to spend with his new friends and would introduce them around Lakeside Country Club.

Autry laughed as Ferebee stepped off the train, saw the photographer, grabbed an umbrella, and began swinging it like a golf club. Not to be outdone, Trane squatted by Ferebee's side, wadded his handkerchief into something approaching the shape of a ball, and set it atop his right hand, which formed a "tee."

Posing on the platform, they looked off into the distance, pretending to follow Ferebee's drive down a fairway of thick railway ties and forged steel. After a brief chat with Stiles, Ferebee headed for room 4333 at "the Host of the Coast," the fashionable Biltmore Hotel.

Goodwin had been right about the press. They were lapping up Ferebee's story. Through its Los Angeles affiliate KNX, CBS Radio had arranged a 15-minute national interview with Ferebee and Trane.

Stiles and his amicable, inventive, and esteemed adversary Darsie L. Darsie, golf editor of the *Los Angeles Evening Herald Express*, were particularly diligent in their coverage. They leaped into what Stiles wrote was "one of the maddest, craziest yet adventurous feats ever attempted" with a passion that rivaled Ferebee's.

On September 19, Darsie coaxed Ferebee out to Flintridge Country Club on the outskirts of Los Angeles and watched as the writer attempted to play 72 holes in one afternoon. He did it "just to gain a little better conception of what [Ferebee] was attempting," Darsie informed his readers in his popular column, "Green Tee."

After six hours and fifteen minutes of golf, Darsie was fielding the congratulations of astonished Flintridge members when "things started swimming and they brought the Green Tee marathon golfer up the hill in a truck and put him to bed. . . . We're not sure we will ever be the same again."

But Darsie was on hand when Ferebee meandered through several practice rounds at Lakeside and again when his legs cramped during a vigorous practice session at hilly Rancho Park Golf Course. While Dr. Alexander and others in the entourage left the course "considerably worried," Darsie wrote, Ferebee pranced along without any overt sign of pain or discomfort.

When he wasn't swinging a club, Ferebee was determined to help Trane publicize the marathon and, more important, the Turbovac. He attended Trane's campaign kickoff, a series of grand luncheons and elegant dinners for Southern California–based contractors, architects, and engineers. There, the attributes of the Turbovac were extolled over thick filet mignons, potatoes, vegetables, salad, and bottles of wine, followed by cherries jubilee for dessert.

The two men followed up a late-night escapade at the Ambassador Hotel's Cocoanut Grove by sliding behind the grill at the Brown Derby one morning. Donning chef's hats, they cooked flapjacks for dozens of hungry customers while photographers fired away. After being introduced to an appreciative crowd, the two went out back, where Trane and a couple of nonplussed waitresses stood over

Ferebee and watched him pretend to hit balls that someone placed under the "brim" of the derby.

Gene Autry made good on his promise to Alexander. After following Ferebee during one of his 72-hole warm-ups Autry took the group on a tour of Los Angeles. He joined everyone at Grauman's Chinese Theatre, which kept customers fresh and cool with a massive air-conditioning unit filled with Trane-manufactured parts. Autry even tried to play a little golf with Ferebee during one practice session at Lakeside, but he surrendered, joking that he'd have to saddle up Champion to keep pace.

Meanwhile, back in Chicago, workers at Municipal Airport were transforming one of the most significant planes in commercial aviation history into a flying billboard for Trane, Ferebee, and the World's Fair.

During a $300 long-distance call in May 1935, American Airlines president Cyrus R. Smith had convinced Donald Douglas of the Douglas Aircraft Company to modify one of his existing planes so that his airline could institute flights offering customers luxury sleeping accommodations. Smith followed the two-hour conversation by wiring Douglas an order for ten planes and a check for $795,000.

With great fanfare, the *Flagship Illinois* was the first of two DC-3 Douglas Sleeper Transports simultaneously introduced to the public by American Airlines on June 26, 1936.

Immediately upon delivery, American Airlines' new planes became the standard for exclusive air travel. The Skysleeper carried 14 overnight passengers and between 21 and 28 "day" travelers, with the interior of the plane divided into eight sections. Two seats in each section folded to form a lower berth, and the upper berth folded down from the ceiling. Directly behind the cockpit was a large space dubbed the "Honeymoon Hut." Every berth featured a thick down mattress. Curtains accorded all the passengers their privacy. Newly developed sound-absorbing material lined the walls, making the Skysleeper the quietest form of transportation available at the time.

Douglas designed a separate lavatory and a dressing room that also served as a small cargo bin in the rear of the plane, next to which was the first hot kitchen facility in U.S. aviation history. In his book *The Legacy of the DC-3*, author Henry Holden writes that American stewardesses now could offer passengers cheese omelets or blueberry pancakes for breakfast; fried chicken, peas, and mashed potatoes for lunch; or duckling à l'orange or filet mignon for supper, with ice cream for dessert—all prepared on board. The food was served on Syracuse china on white damask tablecloths.

The Chicago maintenance crew readied the Skysleeper plane for its new assignment. Workers stripped off the *Flagship Illinois* signage from above the windows and replaced it with lettering that read *The TRANE of the Air* and *The Ferebee Air Conditioned Transcontinental Air Express*. Painted beneath the windows, running from the cockpit to barely beyond the wings, was the line *Destination, Worlds Fair Grounds, New York*. No one noticed that "Worlds" was missing an apostrophe.

Fred Pederson, one of Trane's public relations men, remained behind another few days to oversee the shipment of 75,000 souvenir toy airplanes. They were headed not only to the eight cities on the marathon trail but to 70 other Trane outposts in the United States, Canada, Mexico, South America, Australia, the Philippines, and China. Other cartons contained thousands of multicolored golf balls with "Trane of the Air" and "J. Smith Ferebee" imprinted on them.

Both the toy airplanes and golf balls would be tossed into the crowds that awaited Ferebee at the airports or on the golf courses. Eight balls were painted gold, one reserved for each city. Trane immediately would give the person lucky enough to grab one a crisp $100 bill.

The plane touched down at Grand Central Air Terminal in Glendale, just three miles from the Lakeside course, on September 22. It was immediately transported to Pershing Square across from the Biltmore, where it attracted hordes of curious LA residents, who snooped around inside and out.

Meanwhile, Ferebee attracted attention wherever he went. After a five-hour practice session at Lakeside, Ferebee and Trane were the guests of honor at a luncheon thrown by Harry Brand, the head of publicity for Twentieth Century-Fox and one of Hollywood's most powerful executives.

The year before, Brand had changed Clark Gable's life forever. He convinced Ed Sullivan, then covering Hollywood for the *Chicago Tribune-New York Daily News* syndicate, to run a public opinion poll to name the king and queen of Hollywood. Gable won, and the nickname "King" stuck with him the rest of his career.

As soon as Harry Ritz finished entertaining the luncheon crowd with his wild-eyed antics, Brand introduced Ferebee and Trane to George Marshall, director of Bobby Jones's wildly popular 1931 short movie series, *How I Play Golf*.

Marshall was impressed by Ferebee's conditioning, personality, and good looks and quickly arranged for a screen test. *Chicago Evening American* columnist Ed Cochrane, in Los Angeles to officiate the Southern Cal–Alabama football game that weekend, heard about it. He tossed together a column that proffered "while he is no Clark Gable with the fairer sex, [Ferebee] rates all right."

At the same time, the pre-marathon publicity spurred a small mountain of mail from the public, some of which Ferebee kept for the rest of his life. Mr. T. Redmond Flood of Los Angeles, for fifty years a self-proclaimed walking fanatic, wrote that he was dropping by the Biltmore with several packages of Cur-A-Ped, a product Ferebee knew nothing about. Using the cream liberally, Mr. Flood assured Ferebee, was the only way his feet would hold up throughout the marathon. Ferebee accepted the gift and would soon be grateful for Flood's generosity.

Several other letter writers reminded Ferebee that he was placing undue stress on himself and jeopardizing the marathon by traveling from Los Angeles to New York instead of the other way around. Someone even calculated the time Ferebee would save down to the minute and implored him to reverse his field.

Ferebee graciously responded to all of the correspondence, although he wasn't completely truthful. He explained that New York was dictating how and where the marathon would conclude. He assured folks that he was aware it would be easier to travel from east to west but that he was taking the more difficult path out of a spirit of sportsmanship. He never mentioned the $1,000 payment Goodwin had negotiated from the World's Fair.

One of his favorite missives came from E. L. Paterson of Chicago. Paterson admitted that his only reason for writing to a complete stranger was his deep-seated fear that Ferebee was one of those people who just didn't know when to quit and soon would be "cleaned out." Paterson pleaded, "I just want to see you keep what you've earned."

That entreaty sounded similar to what Angie would have written or said, had she been speaking to her husband. Alone, back in their Chicago home, all Angie knew of Smitty was what she read in the papers.

Reports about Ferebee were plenty. Darsie L. Darsie and Maxwell Stiles continued to monitor Ferebee's every move. Two days before the marathon, Darsie described with great admiration how Ferebee had played 72 holes at Lakeside, jumped into the pool, swam for an hour, took an hour-long massage, and looked "fresh as a daisy" as he contemplated how to spend the afternoon.

Meanwhile, Stiles watched Ferebee and wrote that he would easily win the bet. It would be both a blessing and a curse, he predicted, because while the land and the money would be his, he would never be allowed to escape the marathon madness he'd created.

"He will be besieged with challenges from any number of individuals who claim various legs on the title of champion marathon golfer," Stiles wrote. "All who can afford an airplane as a means of transportation will be out there trying to better Ferebee by playing 700 holes in three days, or something of the like."

Around midnight on Saturday, September 24, The Tall Man went outside, unlocked the side door to the Sharp Stick, and drank a beer while he waited. Within minutes, the door opened and three men walked in.

"Thompson, Jacobs, Campanella, glad to see you could make it," The Tall Man greeted, pointing to the beer. "Have one on me."

A moment later, a few more men arrived.

"Hello, Levin. Hello, Halloran," The Tall Man said cheerfully. "Esposito, you surprise me. I didn't think we'd be seeing you."

A few minutes later, everyone was there. Of the dozen invitations The Tall Man had issued, ten men had formed syndicates made up of their friends, families, and coworkers and raised $200.

The Tall Man took a wide roll of white paper and, with help, tacked it to a wall. Across the top, about a foot apart, The Tall Man had already written the numbers 1, 2, 3, 4. One by one, the men approached, handed him $200, and carefully wrote their names down the left side of the banner: Thompson, Jacobs, Campanella, Levin, Halloran, Esposito, O'Brien, Lacy, Jefferson, and Weisman.

When Weisman was finished, The Tall Man raised his bottle of beer to offer a toast. "To Ferebee," he proclaimed.

Before dawn the next morning, Ferebee stood on the first tee of the Lakeside Golf Club, intent on discouraging anyone from challenging his prowess at endurance golf ever again. Assisted by volunteers carrying flashlights, he began 84 holes by driving a luminous ball into the darkness of the first fairway at 5 a.m.

Lakeside was much more than a place for Bob Hope and Bing Crosby to hang their hats when they left the road. Located only 3½ miles from the heart of Hollywood, the property was a stone's throw from motion-picture sets but maintained the quiet atmosphere of a country estate. From the day it opened on November 14, 1925, the course was considered a shining example of what would come to be known as the Golden Age of Golf Design in Southern California.

Designed by Max Behr, a prolific golf writer and first editor of *Golf Illustrated* magazine whose construction philosophy was to find the right piece of property and then get out of nature's way, par-68 Lakeside ran only about 6,100 yards long and offered but a single par 5.

"Experience has taught us that courses constructed with no higher end than merely to create playgrounds around which one may strike a ball present the golfer with little more than a landscape brutalized with the ideas of some other golfer," Behr once wrote.

Following that philosophy didn't mean the course was easy. From the beginning, Behr, a 1905 graduate of Yale University, designed holes with open fairways and greens with numerous potential pin placements.

At Lakeside, Behr envisioned a links-style course in which he would weave together the property's rolling sand dunes, mature peach and walnut trees, and dried streambeds. He set up five holes to be played over the rapidly dying Los Angeles River. Greens were subtly contoured and demanded accurate approach shots.

The back nine offered a seaside look and feel. Behr eschewed the use of bunkers, opting instead to incorporate the land's natural undulations to protect greens that may have been the first in Southern California made of bentgrass.

In its opening review, the *Los Angeles Times* referenced Lakeside's many "agreeable surprises." Among them was a complete lack of rough. Behr didn't believe in it, and he worked diligently to ensure that his courses didn't need it.

Ferebee's playing in the dark lent an air of surreal theatricality to the start of the marathon, but it did nothing to help his score. After opening with a bogey 5, he immediately added a quadruple-bogey 8 on the second hole and followed that with a double-bogey 6 on number 3.

The remainder of the front nine was only marginally better. He shot a collection of 4s, 5s, and 6s that totaled 12-over-par 47.

Ferebee began the back nine with a horrific triple-bogey 7 and later added a double-bogey 6. But the rest of his showing was more than respectable: five bogeys, two pars, and a birdie 2. At 6:08 a.m., or 68 minutes after his opening shot, Ferebee finished at 19-over-par 89.

With Caschetta on the bag, his second round was only marginally better. He shot an 86 in near solitude in an hour and seven minutes. Autry showed up to watch Ferebee start the third round, while fellow cowpokes Smiley Burnette, Andy Devine, stars Richard Arlen, William Powell, Johnny Weissmuller, Al Jolson, and actress Gail Patrick also wandered in. Fresh and pumped with adrenaline with his new Hollywood pals present to root him on, Ferebee began his third 18 by galloping down the fairways. The stars and starlets hustled to keep up, enthralled by this golf-turned-choreography.

Ferebee would slam a shot and take off. Caschetta, a lightweight bag over his shoulder, matched him step for step. He shouted questions to the forecaddies about upcoming yardages and pulled the appropriate club from his bag so that Ferebee could hit his next shot with hardly a moment's hesitation.

Andy Devine had bet Ferebee $5,000 that he wouldn't be able to traverse Lakeside four times on foot. He stared in disbelief as the stockbroker concluded his third round in an hour and three minutes with a score of 89.

For the fourth round, Ferebee stopped only long enough to change shoes and drink some juice before racing to the first tee and dropping a ball. In an hour and 19 minutes, he was through, putting together nines of 42 and 44 to post his second 86 of the day. Feeling spry and wanting to put a dent in the extra holes he would need to reach 600, Ferebee went back to the 10th tee and reeled off an additional 12 holes in barely 53 minutes, adding 56 strokes.

Before Autry and the other studio stars had finished their wild, raucous cheering, Ferebee flipped the putter to Caschetta and moved toward the clubhouse. He showered, changed into what was to become his trademark bright white slacks and short-sleeve shirt, and raced to a waiting automobile.

He arrived at Grand Central Air Terminal within 12 minutes. After tossing Trane's promotional golf balls into the crowd, he waved an appreciative good-bye from inside the door of the DC-3.

Los Angeles: 84 holes—89-86-89-86-56-406

Two hours later, Ferebee encountered hundreds of fanatics waiting for him when the DC-3 touched down at Sky Harbor Airport in Phoenix. They refused to stay away, despite careless, lukewarm advance coverage by the local papers. The *Arizona Republic* consistently misspelled Ferebee's name in headlines and copy, adding an extra *r*. The day that Ferebee was scheduled to arrive in Phoenix, columnist Les

Hegele proclaimed that competing for $100,000 and a farm in Virginia was time wasted. Playing off the morning's top story of Hitler and the threat of war, Hegele thrust Ferebee into the international arena.

"Why, he could go after big stuff—get Hitler to take up the challenge," Hegele offered. "Now, that's a marathon idea. Ferrebee [*sic*] marathoning against Hitler for several chunks of Czechoslovakia. That would be hilarity plus, having a seat on the 50-yard line for that battle.

"Wouldn't Adolf's face be red when, to the accompaniment of 'heils,' he dubbed a drive and lost half of Sudetenland."

Phoenix Gazette columnist Larry Grill reprised the question of Ferebee's potential earnings from the marathon. He'd "heard" that it might be considerably more than some parcel of land in Virginia. Norbert Downey, another Trane public relations worker, met with Grill and categorically denied that anything more than the farm was at stake.

"Most people can't believe it," Downey told Grill, "but there are no angles to this. . . . It's an amazing sporting proposition, and nothing else."

A thunderous roar went up when Lillian Fette opened the plane door and Ferebee and Trane stood atop some steps that the American Airlines ground crew hurriedly rolled into place. Having been alerted to the importance of brevity, Mayor Walter J. Thalheimer quickly hushed the crowd and the six members of the Chamber of Commerce who were standing behind him and presented Ferebee with the keys to the city. He joked how sad it was that Ferebee wouldn't be in town long enough to use them.

After Ferebee vowed to return, Pederson handed him the bucket of commemorative golf balls. After flinging them into the crowd, he scampered onto the back of a hook-and-ladder truck for a six-mile ride to the Encanto Golf Course that was reminiscent of a Keystone Kops routine.

Motorcycle police led the way, sirens blasting. With his legs tucked around the top rung of the ladder, his head down to deflect the dirt and pebbles flying off the pavement, and his hair billowing in every direction, Ferebee frantically clung to the ladder's sides while Phoenicians waved from the sidewalks below. The truck careened through the streets of downtown until mercifully arriving at the Chamber of Commerce building on West Adams Street for another short ceremony.

Then it was on to Encanto, the city's first municipal course and only the third golf course built in Arizona. At a mere 6,000 yards, Encanto is a marathoner's dream: flat, hard, and surrendering consistently generous rolls. Although small palm trees were planted throughout the property, few of them came into play. Most important for Ferebee, he only had to take a few steps to get from one green to the next tee.

But the course offered practically no shade, and the temperature had zoomed into the high 90s without a cloud in the sky when Ferebee began play at 1:58 p.m. Running after each shot, taking clubs from his forecaddies, and repeating the same rhythmic swing over and over again, Ferebee dazzled a gallery that had been forewarned properly about his ordinary golf skills.

He made birdie on the opening hole, a par-5 of 485 yards that doglegged to the left, when his pitch stopped about five feet from the hole. And while he found enough trouble to finish the opening 18 at 9-over-par 79, Ferebee added three more birdies in jetting around the course in barely 63 minutes. After a change of clothing and a drink, he completed the second 18 in a mere 73 minutes, shooting 83.

Meanwhile, Trane emerged from his banquet meeting with Phoenix-area builders and architects and decided he'd shadow his friend around the course during the third round. His tie flapping in a self-created breeze, he kept his shirt-sleeves still buttoned at the wrist. The air-conditioning magnate playfully wagered five dollars that he'd reach his friend's shots before Ferebee did.

Each time it happened, Trane would chirp, "Another fiver!" Then he'd ask the spectators lined two deep at the greens, "What's wrong with this young fella that I'm beating him down the fairway?"

But Trane was done in by the heat after nine holes. Shirt drenched with sweat, he retreated to the locker room in search of a shower and something dry to wear. Meanwhile, Ferebee completed a third-round score of 79 in one hour and 14 minutes.

Ferebee kept plugging, though at a slightly slower speed and an ever-increasing number of strokes. He had recently finished his fourth full round in 75 minutes, with a high score of 88, when the first leg cramp hit. Dr. Alexander immediately began a vigorous massage of Ferebee's right calf and took a rag soaked in cold water and draped it around the back of his neck.

Yet stopping was out of the question. Trailed by mobile floodlights, Ferebee tacked on another nine holes and 41 strokes before finally finishing Encanto at 7:48 p.m. and in near solitude. Shortly thereafter, he slumped down next to Alexander on the DC-3 and closed his eyes while Lillian Fette readied Ferebee's favorite meal: fried chicken with mashed potatoes and salad, ice tea, and strawberry ice cream for dessert.

As the plane ripped down the runway, Fred Tuerk reached for another air-sickness bag. He was sick, tired, and already $5,000 poorer after losing his bet with Barney Johnson that he could match Ferebee step for step. Fat Fred's only consolation was his view of Dr. Alexander kneeling at Ferebee's feet and feverishly trying to knead the pain from the golfer's right leg.

Phoenix: 81 holes—79-83-79-88-41-370

The Oceana High School basketball team from 1923. Front row, far left, is guard James Smith Ferebee. (Virginia Military Institute Archives)

Ferebee leads his entourage around Olympia Fields Country Club on August 5, 1938, the day he won his original bet with Fred Tuerk by playing 144 holes. (Virginia Military Institute Archives)

Ferebee, caddie Art Caschetta (white shirt, cap, and towel), and a group of caddies and spectators slog through the slop at Olympia Fields on August 5, 1938, the day of the original 144-hole wager. (Virginia Military Institute Archives)

[Top] Ferebee (*seated*) accepts congratulations from Tuerk after completing their 144-hole bet on August 5, 1938, at Olympia Fields Country Club. (Virginia Military Institute Archives)

[Left] Ferebee and Tuerk share a ride atop an elephant in this 1938 photo. Following the 144-hole bet at Olympia Fields, the two were invited to a golf outing to honor the occasion, and the organizer had the elephant waiting. (Courtesy of George Tuerk)

FEREBEE* DRIVES
GOLDEN CROWN
GOLF BALLS
From COAST to COAST

Ferebee is using Golden Crowns because he likes them.

This is not a paid endorsement. In Ferebee's spectacular exhibition it is of the utmost importance to him to select a ball of proven performance. The fact that he chose the Golden Crown is as fine a compliment as the ball could receive.

Golden Crowns are sold exclusively in Walgreen and Agency stores. Single balls 45c—6 for $2.50.

*J. Smith Ferebee is the famous marathon golfing star of the TRANE TRANSCONTINENTAL GOLF MARATHON, backed by Reuben H. Trane, President of the Trane Co. of La Crosse, Wis., and noted air-conditioning authority.

J. SMITH FEREBEE FLYING
"THE TRANE of the AIR"
AIR-CONDITIONED TRANSCONTINENTAL AIR EXPRESS

ARRIVES: CHICAGO MUNICIPAL AIRPORT
(63rd STREET AND CICERO AVENUE)

11:00 A. M. to 12:00 NOON TUESDAY, SEPT. 27
(WATCH NEWSPAPERS FOR ANY UNAVOIDABLE DELAY)

FREE! 100 SOUVENIR AUTOGRAPHED GOLF BALLS DISTRIBUTED ON FEREBEE'S ARRIVAL AT AIRPORT. COME OUT AND GET ONE!

$200.00 IN CASH GIVEN AWAY! 2 SPECIAL GOLD COLORED GOLF BALLS REDEEMED AT AIRPORT FOR $100.00 EACH. EVERYBODY WELCOME!

We repeat Mr. Ferebee was not paid for this endorsement nor is his venture in any sense a commercial proposition

[Left] The advertisement for Golden Crown golf balls that appeared in a Chicago newspaper following Ferebee's 144-hole marathon in August 1938. Note the text at the bottom reiterates that Ferebee received no money to play the company's balls. Date and newspaper unknown. (Virginia Military Institute Archives)

[Bottom right] Dr. Charles Alexander prepares to fly over Olympia Fields Country Club and drop founder Charles Beach's ashes. December 1937. (Courtesy of Madelyn Alexander)

Angeline Ferebee, taken during her employment at Barney Johnson and Company. (Virginia Military Institute Archives)

At Union Station in Los Angeles, Reuben Trane (*crouching*) pretends to watch a shot Ferebee has just hit with the handle of an umbrella. September 17, 1938. (*Los Angeles Examiner*, courtesy of Virginia Military Institute Archives)

Ferebee, Trane (*center*), and Caschetta pose outside the doorway to the American Airlines DC-3 Skysleeper. September 1938. (Courtesy of Trane)

Trane (*left*) and Ferebee cook pancakes at the Brown Derby restaurant on Wilshire Boulevard in Los Angeles during the week of promotions prior to the start of the 600-hole marathon. (Courtesy of Trane)

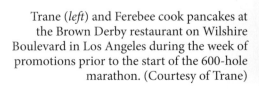

Trane (*left*) and Ferebee pose in front of the *TRANE of the Air*, the American Airlines DC-3 Skysleeper that carried the marathon party from city to city. September 1938. (Courtesy of Trane)

Everyone helps lay in supplies for the big trip. From top left, Trane, Dr. Alexander, and Ferebee pass up loaves of bread handed to them by stewardess Lillian Fette. September 1938. (Virginia Military Institute Archives)

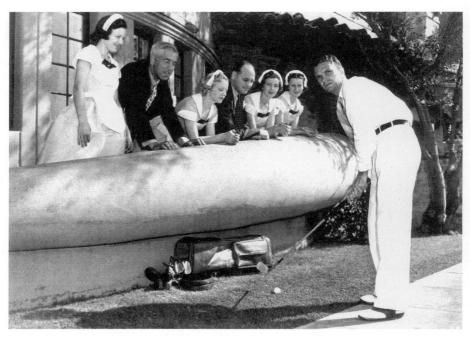

Ferebee plays a shot from under the "brim" of the Brown Derby restaurant on Wilshire Boulevard in Los Angeles, part of the pre-marathon promotions featuring Ferebee and benefactor Reuben Trane. September 1938. (Virginia Military Institute Archives)

Ferebee (*shirtless*) tees off during a practice round at Lakeside Country Club in Burbank, California. Four unidentified caddies keep track of the shot. September 24, 1938. (*Los Angeles Examiner*, courtesy of Virginia Military Institute Archives)

(*From left*) Caschetta, Ferebee, and Trane mug for a photographer during a practice round at Lakeside Country Club in Burbank, California. Date unknown. (*Los Angeles Examiner*, courtesy of Virginia Military Institute Archives)

Actor Arthur Treacher (*left*) enjoys a conversation with Ferebee (*center*) and Trane during the week leading to the start of the golf marathon. September 1938. (Courtesy of Trane)

Ferebee (*left*) and Trane chat with Sid Grauman outside the famous movie theater that carried his name. The Trane Company manufactured many of the parts in the theater's air-conditioning unit. (Courtesy of Trane)

Trane (*left*) and Ferebee share a laugh with Harry Ritz of the Ritz Brothers, probably at the Cocoanut Grove. September 1938. (Courtesy of Trane)

Ferebee climbs aboard a fire truck just off First Avenue in Phoenix for the trip from Sky Harbor Airport to Encanto Golf Course. September 25, 1938. (Courtesy of Trane)

Ferebee (*center*) takes a drink from Dr. Alexander while walking with five unidentified caddies during play at Blue Hills Country Club in Kansas City. September 26, 1938. (*Kansas City Journal-Post*)

(*From bottom*) Dr. Alexander, Ferebee (holding Snowball), and Trane board the DC-3 Skysleeper. This photo may have been taken on September 26, 1938, the day Ferebee adopted Snowball off the Blue Hills Country Club course in Kansas City. (Virginia Military Institute Archives)

The citation that the mayor of Kansas City gave to Ferebee upon his arrival on September 26, 1938. Notice he is referred to as "F. Smith Ferebee." (Virginia Military Institute Archives)

Caschetta, Trane, and Ferebee wave to well-wishers who greeted them at an unidentified airport on their four-day, eight-city marathon stop. (Virginia Military Institute Archives)

[Top] Ferebee followers at Milwaukee's Tuckaway Country Club scramble after the gold-painted golf ball worth $100 was thrown into the crowd by Trane. September 27, 1938. (Courtesy of Trane)

[Right] Under the watchful eye of Fette, Dr. Alexander examines Ferebee's feet on board the DC-3 Skysleeper. September 1938. (Courtesy of Trane)

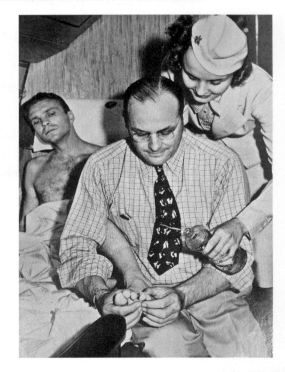

(*From left*) Dr. Alexander, Trane, Ferebee (holding Snowball), and Al Knoebel, the stowaway. Date and location unknown. (Virginia Military Institute Archives)

Two unidentified men follow Ferebee (*center*) and Dr. Alexander (*right*) at Olympia Fields during the 600-hole marathon. September 27, 1938. (Virginia Military Institute Archives)

Ferebee is followed by a tiny entourage of Philadelphians during one of his rounds at North Hills Country Club. September 28, 1938. (Courtesy of Trane)

Ringed by spectators, Ferebee plays the 18th hole at North Hills Country Club in Philadelphia. September 28, 1938. (Virginia Military Institute Archives)

Ferebee tees off into the darkness during one of his final rounds at Salisbury Country Club on Long Island. September 28, 1938. (Virginia Military Institute Archives)

A haggard-looking Ferebee stops for a photo in Newark, New Jersey, with stowaway Al Knoebel (*left front*), Dr. Alexander, Trane, and Fette. September 28, 1938. (Courtesy of Trane)

The *TRANE of the Air* finally lands at Mitchel Field, Long Island, as newsmen rush to get a quote from Ferebee (blocked by man wearing white hat in foreground). That's Reuben Trane (*left foreground*) walking away from the hoopla. (Virginia Military Institute Archives)

Mission accomplished! Ferebee celebrates completion of
600-hole marathon. September
28, 1938. (Virginia Military
Institute Archives)

Ferebee, circa 1943.
(Virginia Military
Institute Archives)

Ferebee, date unknown.
(Virginia Military
Institute Archives)

Lt. James Smith Ferebee in flight regalia. This photo appeared in July 1943 issue of *UPCHECK* magazine, published by the School of Aeronautics, Lockport, Illinois. (Virginia Military Institute Archives)

Ferebee received this photograph of Chick Evans (*left*) and the legendary Bobby Jones, on which Jones wrote, "For J. Smith Ferebee, I am grateful for your many kindnesses and with warmest regards, Bob Jones." Date and location unknown. (Virginia Military Institute Archives)

Ferebee returns a toast made in his honor by U.S. senator John Warner during a banquet in Richmond. Date unknown. (Virginia Military Institute Archives)

Ferebee with President Gerald R. Ford. Date and place unknown. (Virginia Military Institute Archives)

Ferebee with President Ronald Reagan. Date unknown. (Virginia Military Institute Archives)

7

A Snowball's Chance

Ferebee teetered up and down the narrow aisle of the DC-3, accepting congratulations from Trane and the other passengers as the twin-engine plane left Sky Harbor Airport behind. In the cockpit, Capt. Ed Bowe set a course for Kansas City.

The handsome 33-year-old captain had a colorful background, one he retold with such charm and wit that more than one stewardess violated American Airlines' cardinal edict to "not succumb to the temptation of becoming too jovial" with the pilots.

Born in Mineral Wells, Mississippi, Bowe learned to fly during a two-year stint at Mississippi Agricultural and Mechnical (A&M) College. He left school to sell fertilizer and soon discovered that his biggest deals occurred after he took customers for a ride in the two-seat biplane that he affectionately called *Jenny*.

Bowe soon joined Compañía Mexicana de Aviación, transporting payrolls over the Mexican mountains and into oil towns. The men there were far too busy to clear a landing strip; instead, they'd stretch out a huge sheet onto which they'd painted a bull's-eye. Bowe's job was to make sure the bag of gold hit the mark.

In 1929, Bowe returned to the United States to work for the Southern Air Transport System, the precursor to American Airlines. After seven years in Texas, he'd been transferred to Los Angeles, where he'd purchased what he laughingly called a ranch in Manhattan Beach. He played the organ to relax and dreamed of raising chinchillas.

The other American Airlines representative on board was stewardess Lillian Fette. Born in Muenster, Texas, Fette attended a convent school in Wisconsin before switching to Aquinas High School in La Crosse. After two years at Texas Tech

University, she returned to Wisconsin to attend nursing school. Joining American Airlines, she was one of the first stewardesses selected to work on Skysleeper flights and was assigned to Glendale, California.

By 1938, Hollywood had discovered Fette's radiant smile and girl-next-door charm, and her prospects looked more promising on the ground than they did in the air. Not only had she played a stewardess—uncredited—in the Gary Cooper–Merle Oberon movie *The Cowboy and the Lady*, but she'd also been the central figure in a national marketing campaign for Pepsodent toothpaste.

After serving dinner to the other passengers, Fette joined Ferebee and Trane in the rear of the plane. The two men were giddy, congratulating themselves on the quick work they had made of opening day. Once Dr. Alexander wandered back to the table to make sure his patient was feeling okay, Fette moved to the Honeymoon Hut directly behind the cockpit and began converting Ferebee's berth into a sleeper.

Around 11 p.m., Ferebee said good night and pulled the curtain on the Honeymoon Hut, confident that he would awaken refreshed and ready to skip around Blue Hills Country Club in Kansas City.

He might have been right had he actually slept. But Bowe's flight path took the plane through turbulent air pockets that created 100-foot drops in altitude "as quickly as you can snap your fingers," Ferebee later wrote. "It felt like the bed was dropping right out from under me!"

It didn't help matters any that Bowe was forced to refuel in Fort Worth, Texas, resulting in an additional bumpy landing and rocky takeoff that the jittery Ferebee could have done without. The marathon party touched down at Kansas City's Municipal Air Terminal right around five o'clock in the morning. Although spirits remained high, as they left the plane, Ferebee joked with Dr. Alexander that he was "tired when I finished Phoenix, and I'm already dog-tired and I haven't even started Kansas City."

The city exuded a festive mood. As Bowe was piloting the plane eastward, more than 100,000 citizens of Kansas City, proud and grateful, had gathered at Liberty Memorial Mall for Jubilesta, the annual early fall festival to celebrate a bountiful harvest.

Ferebee was met at the airport by city officials and a police motorcade, which provided a harrowing escort to Blue Hills. While Ferebee held on for dear life in the back of a black sedan, the motorcade, its lights flashing and sirens blaring, zoomed to the golf course at 90 miles per hour. It covered a distance that normally took 30 minutes in barely half that time.

Blue Hills was located on what had once been the Elm Ridge racetrack, which had opened at the turn of the century but was shuttered when Missouri outlawed horseracing in 1906. Six years later, some wealthy Missourians opened a country club on that property. They drew its name from the distinct bluish hue of the grass on which the golf course was built.

Members loved playing shots over the remains of what had once been a popular sporting venue. Golfers crossed the old grassy track when playing holes 1, 2, 5, 10, and 12. Number 13 was in the center of what had been the racing oval, while number 15 ran parallel to the track. The 9th and 18th greens stood where the grandstand and paddock once had been.

The prior history of the course led to some confusing exchanges between club caddies and their unaware guests. Well-played shots were hailed for "stopping on top of the race track." Other shots were "short of the track" or "went over the track."

Almost every hole of the 6,200-yard layout was up a hill, down a hill, or followed some combination of the two. After a particularly strenuous round, it wasn't unusual for some of the club's more out-of-shape members and guests to require assistance up the unusually steep, broad stone steps that led from the course through a garden and to a veranda from which the entire grounds could be seen.

The week in Los Angeles had afforded Ferebee the opportunity to play practice rounds at Lakeside, with a side trip to Encanto, before the marathon began. Ferebee didn't have the same advantage at Blue Hills, about which he knew nothing. Thus he implemented a unique suggestion that Caschetta had made about the new courses: Art advised Ferebee to hire a local caddie to guide him through the opening round. In the meantime, Caschetta would run ahead and scout the course, plotting a strategy that hopefully would save time and strokes during the second, third, and fourth rounds.

Ferebee agreed, and Goodwin was told to make the caddie arrangements in Kansas City, St. Louis, Milwaukee, Philadelphia, and New York. After introducing himself to the hired hand at Blue Hills, Caschetta lingered long enough to share a couple of simple tips on what Ferebee expected from the caddie and then dashed off.

Blue Hills was not designed to promote fast starts. The opening two holes were both par 5s, part of an odd front-nine configuration featuring four par 5s and three par 3s. The incoming nine was abnormal in its own way, with seven par 4s.

"The toughest course I've played so far," Ferebee assured inquisitive newsmen following an opening-round 91—18 over par—that began when he teed up a luminous ball at 6:02 a.m. He found trouble right away, scoring a triple-bogey 8 followed by a bogey 6 on number 2. He righted things with pars on four of the next seven holes and started the back nine with a twisting 20-foot putt for a birdie 3.

Then his game collapsed. A triple-bogey 7 on number 11 was followed by double bogeys on the next two holes. He wheezed home with a pair of 5s and a couple of 6s, his confidence greatly strained.

The Blue Hills that Ferebee encountered at six o'clock in the morning was so laden with dew that he was forced to change shoes and socks every few holes. Physically, that slowed his charge. Mentally, it broke his concentration.

But with Caschetta back on the bag for the next three rounds, Ferebee's game quickly improved. Traversing the course for the second time in only an hour and 30 minutes, Ferebee lowered his score by eight shots to finish with a comfortable 83.

His score also matched the early morning temperature. It would hit a high of 95, or a smoldering 19 degrees higher than normal, before he departed for St. Louis.

The third round was Ferebee's best, a 4-over-par 77, with 11 pars and his second birdie of the day on number 10. He also finished in an hour and 15 minutes.

Early in the fourth round, a small white dog wandered onto one of the greens. He delighted a crowd of about 500 people by standing there stoically until Ferebee came into view and took the last few steps up a hill. Then the dog wagged his tail in wild, wide circles that caused half of his body to shake.

"Someone please come and get this dog," Caschetta called out, politely. No one moved.

After watching patiently while Ferebee tapped in, the dog followed the group to the next tee, and its tail continued to spiral madly. Again, Caschetta yelled for help. Again, no one responded.

Three holes in the broiling sun later, Ferebee turned to Dr. Alexander. "Alex, this dog doesn't have a snowball's chance in hell in this heat," he said.

The doctor took his cue, grabbing the pup and offering it some water from a paper cup. Any hope of driving it away ended the moment that the dog's tongue touched the cool liquid and Alexander gave his head a couple of quick strokes.

"Looks like we're taking this little guy with us," Ferebee told Alexander near the end of a fourth-round 82 that consumed only one hour and 20 minutes. "Christ, he's completely fagged."

So was Ferebee, a point Fred Tuerk gleefully made to newsmen. Tuerk had spent the morning inside Blue Hills' posh clubhouse, feasting at the buffet, flipping an occasional nickel into the slot machines, and phoning Chicago to check on his stocks.

"Look at his eyes," Tuerk advised those around him as Ferebee ambled past. "They're completely bloodshot. I'm telling you, he won't last out tomorrow."

Ferebee climbed the stairs to the clubhouse veranda, accepting a bucket filled with 100 of Trane's specially painted golf balls. Below him, the crowd jockeyed for whatever position they guessed would put them in place for the $100 gold ball.

Seconds later, the scramble was on with Francis Waters of Brooklyn Avenue emerging from the pile. Trane handed over a $100 bill, joking that he hoped it was enough to replace the natty, pin-striped suit Waters had ruined while rolling in the grass to snatch the ball. Ferebee smiled and waved congratulations and then hurried inside for a shower and an on-time departure.

"His haggard face visibly showed the strain," an unnamed reporter for the *Kansas City Journal* noted. "With attendants caring for him while the automobile raced to the waiting plane, Ferebee lay back and rested."

Twenty minutes later, Bowe had the *TRANE of the Air* off the ground and on its way to St. Louis. The flight would take only about an hour, giving Ferebee barely enough time to down some lunch and close his eyes.

Stewardess Lillian Fette took Snowball, as Ferebee named the newest passenger, fed him some diced chicken, and then placed him in her berth at the rear of the plane. Within minutes, he was able to do something Ferebee had yet to master while aboard.

He quickly fell asleep.

Kansas City: 72 holes—91-83-77-82-333

People in St. Louis seemed more thrilled to see Ferebee than anywhere he'd played thus far. A huge, enthusiastic throng awaited him at Lambert Field, including Bernard F. Dickmann, who had ridden Franklin Roosevelt's coattails to become the city's first Democratic mayor in 24 years.

The plane touched down. Ferebee and Trane stood at the door and waved to the crowd. Ferebee was then whisked down the stairs to the waiting microphone of radio behemoth KMOX, whose 50,000-watt transmitter tower and clear-channel signal made it one of the first international stations, capable of being heard in New Zealand and the Arctic Circle after dark.

In his only setback thus far, Goodwin had pleaded with the station to interview Ferebee after he played at Norwood Hills Country Club. That would be approximately 8:30 p.m., in effect giving the world a shot at hearing the segment. The station refused his request, so Goodwin settled for a brief, daytime question-and-answer session with reporter Don Phillips.

When Phillips was through, the Ferebee entourage distributed souvenir toy planes to the crowd. One lucky spectator scooped up another golden golf ball and walked away with 100 bucks. Mayor Dickmann then joined Ferebee and Trane in the lead car for the second hair-raising motorcade ride of the day. Twenty minutes later, they arrived at Norwood Hills, a club that had emerged from a troubled beginning to become a cherished local institution.

Initially called North Hills until financial problems forced a reorganization under a new name, sophisticated it was not. Next door sat the Durkin Farm, whose fences were no match for the family's nomadic cows and hogs. Club members soon realized that the best way to make sure that Durkin paid for the inevitable property damage his wandering livestock caused was to hold the animals hostage until the repair work was done. That tactic often required members to play around cows that had been tethered to trees just off the fairway.

Golf at Norwood Hills began in glorious excess in 1923 when an East Course, West Course, and 9-hole South Course opened at the same time. Designed by Wayne Stiles, a landscape architect from Boston, the 45 holes were routed in just 90 days under the manic supervision of Sam Lyle. Ever-present cigarette dangling from his lips, the ashes burrowing pinprick holes in the jackets of his otherwise smart double-breasted suits, Lyle dashed across the 380 acres from one course to another on horseback. Under his command were 250 men, 55 teams of horses, 5 tractors, and 8 five-ton trucks.

One of the oddities of Norwood Hills was its lone slot machine. Located in the pro shop rather than the men's locker room, as was done in most other clubs, the machine didn't pay off in coins. Instead, a winning combination caused golf balls to roll down the chute.

It was 3 p.m. and 100 steamy degrees when Ferebee was introduced on the first tee of the West Course. With Missouri in the middle of a drought, the ground had been baked so hard that Ferebee struggled simply to push his tee into the turf. Several of them broke off in his hand, although local caddie Leo Werne quickly supplied him with a replacement.

It took only an hour and 19 minutes for Ferebee to play the more challenging West Course in 13-over-par 84. A triple-bogey 7 on the medium-length fourth hole was his only major blemish. A gallery of about 500 observers had sprinted behind him following his opening drive, but the people were so exhausted by the heat and the pace he set that almost all of them had quit midway through the front nine.

Jumping over to the East Course, Ferebee polished off the 6,006-yard par 70 in only 8-over-par 78, and in an hour and 27 minutes. After a six-minute break to walk from the 18th green to the first tee and to change his shoes, Ferebee started a second uneventful trip around the West Course at 4:50 p.m. He finished an hour and 27 minutes later with a score of 12-over-par 83.

At 7:18 p.m., Ferebee jumped back to the East Course to begin his final 18 holes. It was dark enough that, as he dashed after his drive on the first hole, two tiny fire department trucks with floodlights mounted on the back followed behind him.

Ferebee was erratic and posted a pokey front-nine score of 45 that consumed nearly an hour. Fighting the onrushing darkness, he opened with a double-bogey 6 on the first hole, followed by bogeys on four of the next five holes. He then closed the front nine with a triple-bogey 7.

The 11th hole of the East Course was a 385-yard descent into hell and back. Ferebee hit his tee shot from atop a dam that quickly dropped off and sloped hard left toward a line of Osage Orange and pine trees before turning sharply back uphill to the green. Another line of trees on the right rendered the average player's landing area in a fairway darker than a cave.

It was after 8:30 p.m. when Ferebee reached the 11th tee, angry at himself after a double-bogey 5 on the previous hole. The two spotlights were trained on the fairway in the vague hope that Ferebee and his forecaddies would easily find his drive.

As Ferebee came off the dam and started down the hill, his left foot caught the edge of a hole. He lost his balance and began tumbling down the steep, narrow trail to the fairway as though he were the largest boulder in an avalanche. Caschetta was closest to him. He lunged and tried to grab his friend's right arm, but he whiffed in the darkness.

With no regard for his own safety, Alexander gave chase, hurtling past Caschetta and down the hill. When he reached the bottom, he found Ferebee writhing in pain and clutching his right ankle.

"It's not broken," the doctor told him after a quick exam, "but it's sprained, a bad sprain."

While Alexander tended to Ferebee, newsmen riding on the back of the fire trucks quickly hopped off and ran to the clubhouse to phone their papers. It didn't take long for the news to reach Chicago, though the severity of Ferebee's injury was unknown.

The Tall Man was finishing a phone call when his 10 adversaries walked into the side room of the Sharp Stick. Reluctantly, he relayed the news he'd recently received about Ferebee's frightening spill and how he had limped badly through the final few holes.

As he feared, the 10 men immediately sought to take the buyout and settle for a $25 profit. Except that as far as The Tall Man was concerned, Ferebee's injury negated the opportunity for any of them to opt out of the bet.

"I've just been told that we won't know until tomorrow whether he's well enough to play," he explained, "and if he can't play, I win. I'm not letting you pull out of here tonight with $225 that tomorrow morning could well be mine.

"But if Ferebee starts play in the morning, you can pull out then, just like we agreed. But you had better be ready with an answer as soon as I know something. So if you need to talk to the others, you had better do it now."

The room quickly emptied. What a stroke of good fortune, The Tall Man thought. The injury dramatically increased his odds of beating these guys out of a couple thousand dollars.

He would have felt even more confident had he read the quotes Tuerk provided newspapermen in St. Louis after Ferebee finished.

"Look at the way he's limping around," Fat Fred crowed. "I'm not worried about this. He'll be done soon enough."

While finishing play, Ferebee did his best to act as though nothing unusual had happened. When he discovered that someone had left his final change of clothes on the airplane, Ferebee quipped that he'd sign an autograph for anyone who would lend him any item that fit.

Over the next hour, he signed everything from one of Norwood Hills' monogrammed cloth napkins to a crisp dollar bill. When he finally had obtained an outfit, he went inside to shower. Then, against all advice, he insisted on eating a leisurely dinner with the six local youngsters who had caddied for him. They finally finished around 11 p.m. Imploring those who remained at the club to "keep your fingers crossed for me," Ferebee signaled Trane and Caschetta and gingerly made his way to the car.

"Doing just fine," he shouted to some people in the parking lot.

Only a fool would have believed it.

Waiting anxiously on the plane for Ferebee was Dr. Alexander, eager to conduct a more thorough examination. When he had finished, it was clear that in addition to the sprained ankle, Ferebee had incurred some minor ligament damage to his right knee.

Considering the nature of the fall, it could have been worse. Ferebee would experience some pain, but Alexander assured him that he would do everything in his power to make sure Ferebee finished the marathon.

"It's not his leg that I'm worried about," Alexander later confided to Trane. "It's the combination of pain, his lack of sleep, and the next 291 holes that makes me wonder whether we are doing right by the guy."

St. Louis: 72 holes—84-78-83-87-332

8

Midwest Madness

Brooding over what was shaping up to be his third consecutive sleepless night, Ferebee was staring at the ceiling of the Honeymoon Hut when Capt. Ed Bowe's loud, throaty curse from the cockpit sliced through the dual drone of propeller engines. It was 2 a.m., and Bowe had just been told that Milwaukee's Municipal Airport was closed.

Ferebee's once-rigid schedule was in tatters following the developments in St. Louis. First, his leg injury had slowed the final round dramatically. Then there was his playful, though ill-advised, decision to swap autographs for clothing at Norwood Hills, compounded by his even more curious insistence on dining with the club's caddies. Judging from the anger in Bowe's voice, the bill for those mishaps and mistakes had just come due.

Even so, Bowe kept the DC-3 on course, hoping he might cajole someone in Milwaukee to let him land. But no matter how ardently he negotiated, coaxed, and, finally, begged, nothing changed. The facility was shut down for the night. Bowe would have to take his plane somewhere else for a few hours and come back.

The only airport that made sense was Municipal Airport in Chicago. After calling Trane to the front and explaining the situation, the exasperated pilot turned the DC-3 northward and found a safe haven. On the ground, without any turbulence bouncing him all over the place, Ferebee actually enjoyed about three hours of sleep before being jolted awake when Bowe cranked the engines again.

At dawn, the *TRANE of the Air* was hovering back over Milwaukee, this time with permission to land.

Even though there were still four cities on the itinerary, not to mention 291 grueling holes of golf, Milwaukee stood as a celebratory stop of sorts. Given the city's proximity to Trane's headquarters in La Crosse, large numbers of employees were expected to be on hand at the airport and at the Tuckaway Country Club.

In addition to the usual party Trane hosted for architects and engineers at the clubs where Ferebee played, several other small, rapid-fire engagements took place, and all members of the traveling party were invited. Except Ferebee and Caschetta, that is. Escorted by deputy sheriffs on motorcycles, the two men jumped into a waiting car and sped off for the course, arriving shortly after sunup. About 30 early risers had already gathered there, including peeved club president Thomas Millane.

Led to believe that Ferebee would be zooming through the gates to Tucka-way while it was still dark and that he wished to start playing before dawn, Millane had arranged for several portable floodlights to be brought onto the course. Now that they weren't needed, he was none too happy.

As with any club, Tuckaway had its quirks. To be eligible for membership, one had to own stock in the Meyrose Land Corporation, named for a German family that had amassed countless acres of swampland in the mid-1800s for only a couple of dollars an acre. Henry Meyrose had learned something in northwestern Germany that set him apart from other Greenfield, Wisconsin, residents—that is, how to drain marshes and transform them into usable property.

Soon after the club opened in 1924, Tuckaway's Board of Directors discovered that limiting membership to those who could afford both stock in Meyrose and the $75 annual club dues offered no assurance of a proper level of gentility. Over the years, members had developed a peculiar game. Ginger ale glasses were smuggled into the locker room by the dozen and then tossed into the shower area to see who could hit the most showerheads. Cleaning broken glass from the shower floor soon became the locker-room attendant's most precarious chore, which Tuckaway board members were regularly reminded had never been mentioned in the job interview. Neither was the fact that the help staff was housed in what a board member once bemoaned was an "outhouse in which very few self-respecting men would live."

Some club members were notorious for appearing unannounced in the dining room with 20 or 30 friends and immediately expecting to feast on gourmet meals. No matter how many beleaguered chefs stormed away never to return, the message never completely got through to these members that no kitchen regularly stocked that quantity or quality of food. Other members, who were equally inconsiderate, made dinner party reservations for 25 or 30 then never bothered to show up or to cancel.

Tuckaway was not the celebratory stop the Ferebee party had imagined. Outside of the Trane employees and a handful of club members, Milwaukee appeared singularly unimpressed and uninterested in Ferebee. The largest crowd estimates were placed at about 200 people, and it was noted that most of them hovered around the clubhouse. Spectators were so scarce that a cop who had been brought in for security caught the $100 golden golf ball Ferebee tossed out when he was through playing.

Perhaps an Associated Press photo that had appeared in the papers the day before his arrival fed their indifference. Under the headline *Ferebee Seems to Enjoy His Trip,* Smitty stood in the doorway of the *TRANE of the Air* with his arm draped around sweet, smiling stewardess Lillian Fette. Both were waving and sporting ear-to-ear grins. The first sentence of the caption beneath the photo read, "Judging by this picture, J. Smith Ferebee's transcontinental golf marathon isn't all 'grind.'"

By the time Milwaukee reporters had their first look at Ferebee's real condition and relayed to their readers the duress under which he was performing, it was too late to drum up sympathy.

The *Milwaukee News* ran two photos of Ferebee taken at Tuckaway. In the first, he was standing between caddie Art Caschetta and Henry Gavre, the local caddie they'd hired. Clearly, Ferebee was limping along beside them. The next photo showed Dr. Alexander kneeling in front of Ferebee, treating his ankle and badly blistered feet.

Lloyd Larson of the *Milwaukee News* painted the same picture of Ferebee in words after watching his first of more than four rounds at Tuckaway. Ferebee, Larson wrote, "ran, walked, ambled and stumbled" around the golf course.

With his right leg heavily taped and the "high spots" on his feet bandaged, Ferebee jogged into the clubhouse and immediately encountered Tuckaway professional Burle Gose. The two men stared at each other in disbelief; their faces could have been those of identical twins. Gose was slightly shorter and chunkier than Ferebee, whose weight had plunged 10 pounds to 150 in just two days.

Gose politely offered Ferebee a couple of quick pointers about his golf course. It featured a par-70 that was barely 6,000 yards long and unfolded like a garden hose. The front nine was bunched in a tight circle in the center of the property. The back nine formed a ring around the outside. Water came into play on only three holes, most prominently on number 18, a severe dogleg-right that measured 375 yards. Some holes were snuggled inside heavy pockets of trees; others offered absolutely no obstacles from the tee to the green.

Overall, Tuckaway presented little challenge for Ferebee—until it was time to putt. As with any championship course of shorter length, the primary manner used to protect par was to construct greens with subtle breaks and undulations that could only be learned through experience. Generally a deft putter whose short game was strong, Ferebee grew frustrated as he found himself three-putting about half of the holes.

Guided by the local caddie while Caschetta scouted the course, Ferebee completed his first round in 83 minutes, shooting 80. A Milwaukee wire service scribe quickly filed a story that immediately was transmitted across the nation.

At the Sharp Stick, The Tall Man made his daily phone call and was informed that Ferebee had resumed play. With him in the side room were the 10 syndicate representatives. He told them that not only had Ferebee played his first round, but also that he had shot a most respectable score of 80 and was continuing to play.

"Does anyone want out?" he asked.

The Tall Man was surprised when only two men, Campanella and Levin, stepped forward. He quickly paid them each $225, their share minus the $25 pull-out fee, and turned to those who remained.

"You people either have guts or are desperate," he said, certain he already knew the answer.

Ferebee was even faster, though not as accurate, the second time around Tuckaway. With Caschetta on the bag, he covered 18 holes in 61 minutes, but shot 84.

Forced to change socks and shoes after each round in a losing battle against blisters, Ferebee saw his scores and his times increase alarmingly. He took an hour and 12 minutes and 86 strokes to complete his third round, and an hour and 24 minutes and 87 shots to complete the fourth round. He then completed three additional par-4 holes, numbers 10–12, leaving him with 72 holes to play in Chicago, Philadelphia, and New York.

"I feel swell, but I've got a long way to go on these dogs," he yelled to the crowd before slipping inside the Tudor-style clubhouse for a shower. "So, please, hold your thumbs up for me."

Later, as Ferebee ducked into the car and the driver started the engine, forecaddie Richard Dzioba tried to approach him. A policeman, thinking the teenager wanted an autograph, shoved him back.

"Sir, I've got it!" Dzioba screamed, waving a gold watch in the air.

Ferebee quickly emerged from the car and took the timepiece, which had been a gift from Olympia Fields members following the 144-hole marathon. It had fallen from his pocket at some point during the second round, and Ferebee had glumly presumed it was lost.

But Dzioba had refused to give up the hunt. While Ferebee prepared to leave, he scoured the course and finally found the watch in the tall rough bordering the long par-5 second hole. Impressed with the young man's tenacity, Trane handed him a crisp 100-dollar bill.

Ferebee marveled at the good fortune of having his watch returned. As he sat back and busied himself polishing it with his handkerchief, the car careened back to the airport. There, another surprise was waiting.

Milwaukee: 75 holes—80-84-86-87-14-351

As soon as he stepped onto the plane, Lillian Fette informed him that a telegram had arrived while he was playing Tuckaway. She had placed it on his table in the Honeymoon Hut.

It was from Angie, who had spent the morning with Ferebee's brother Enoch in Chicago. They had been walking past the Tribune Building on Michigan Avenue when they learned of his injury in St. Louis.

Worried for you -(STOP)- Coming to airport -(STOP)- Need company? -(STOP)- Love Angie

Ferebee hobbled to the rear of the plane, where Trane and Dr. Alexander were huddling. Sheepishly, Ferebee told them about the telegram. He asked whether Trane would mind adding one more passenger.

Before the industrialist could answer, Alexander joked that since Ferebee didn't seem to like sleeping on airplanes, it might be good to have someone else on board who would be interested in one of his all-night conversations.

Trane understood Alexander's gambit and played along. Neither man wanted Ferebee to know about their doubts that he would finish. If having Angie aboard would distract him from the pain, fine. A return to some semblance of marital harmony couldn't hurt, either.

"Of course, she's welcome, but only if you two promise to behave yourself up there," Trane playfully admonished, pointing in the direction of the Honeymoon Hut. "The way you're playing, you're going to need every ounce of strength you can muster."

It wasn't until the plane was well away from Milwaukee that Snowball heard a noise in the dressing room and began barking. Fred Pederson opened the door and discovered a young boy crouched behind a stack of large sacks filled with dirty laundry. Grabbing the slender stowaway, who appeared to be no more than 15 or 16 years old, Pederson dragged him before Ferebee and Trane.

Particularly perturbed, Trane asked for the boy's name.

"Al."

"Al what?" Trane snapped back, even more annoyed at having to drag information out of the kid.

"Knoebel," he replied softly, pulling a black cap off his head.

"And?" Trane was now glowering at the intruder.

Reluctantly, the boy confessed that he'd been following Ferebee's progress in the papers. He lived near the Milwaukee airport and had dropped by, intending only to get a glimpse of the flamboyant marathoner during his brief visit. Hanging near the back of a small crowd of gawkers who were invited to look around the plane, Al watched as Lillian Fette took a telegram to the Honeymoon Hut. Almost without thinking, he had quietly opened the door to the dressing room and slipped inside unnoticed.

"Look, mister, I really didn't plan this," he told Trane. "You don't believe me? Then how come the only clothes I've got are on my back?"

Ferebee was battling so many other issues—a lack of sleep and his inflamed leg, swollen hands, and foot blisters—that he couldn't have cared less about the kid. But he offered Trane a quick solution to the problem: put Al in charge of Snowball, and have someone contact his mother when they landed in Chicago to explain what had happened.

"Tell her we'll make sure he gets home fine once this is over," Ferebee said. "And tell her not to worry; we won't press charges."

Then he turned to the intruder. "Two bits of advice for you: don't get in trouble, and take good care of that dog," he warned. "Other than that, stay out of the goddamned way."

Chicago, meanwhile, had prepared a welcome fit for a hero. Waiting at the airport was Mayor Edward J. Kelly and members of the New Century Committee, a nonprofit organization that had been formed to stimulate business and culture in the city.

The committee had enticed the Packard dealership on South Michigan Avenue to provide an open-air car that would whisk Ferebee to Olympia Fields at precisely 11:42 a.m. It also had arranged a police escort to make sure the trip went smoothly. Likewise, it had prepared for the possibility that Ferebee wouldn't finish four rounds at Olympia Fields until after dark. Fire Department commissioner Michael J. Corrigan had made a floodlight truck available to the club.

At Olympia Fields, the party was in full swing when the caravan arrived at 12:08 p.m. Ferebee's competitive nemesis, Adam J. Riffel, was chairman of the club's Sports and Pastimes Committee. He assessed Ferebee's situation and the city's ebullient response and saw in both the opportunity to give the club some badly needed exposure.

He suggested that September 27 be declared "Smith Ferebee Day" and that Olympia Fields celebrate by opening its doors to anyone, members and nonmembers alike. The public was invited to play any of the club's four courses, with the hope that enough would enjoy the experience to apply for membership.

The only caveat, an obvious one, was that the golfers had to abide by the course marshals' admonition to step to the side any time Ferebee came within one hole of their position. Nothing could be allowed to impede his pace of play. Otherwise, the public was welcome to share the feeling with members that they were either witnessing history or participating in it.

Ferebee and Angie hopped into the back of the Packard for a private interlude on the ride to the course. She had packed a suitcase, just in case, and she eagerly accepted her husband's invitation to join him for the rest of the trip. She never asked for an apology; he never offered one.

Goodwin had told officials in Milwaukee that Ferebee was being accompanied by two airplanes filled with Chicago-based reporters, broadcasters, and newsreel photographers. If it was ever true, it certainly wasn't now.

Under recently promoted manager Gabby Hartnett, the Chicago Cubs had risen from nowhere to within 1½ games of the National League's leader, the Pittsburgh Pirates. With just six games to play, the Pirates were at Wrigley Field for a three-game series that almost certainly would decide the pennant. Chicago was aflame with baseball fever. That fact might have curtailed Ferebee's press cover-age, but it didn't stop hundreds of people from roaming the fairways at Olympia Fields. They seemed to be having a great time testing their luck.

Outsiders meandered through the clubhouse. Some stopped to hear Bob Elson's radio broadcast of lame-armed Dizzy Dean valiantly battling the Pirates, or as *Chicago Evening American* columnist Ed Cochrane had begun calling them, the "Jitter-bucs."

Ferebee, of course, had his own race to complete. Whereas he had begun the 144-hole marathon in August on Olympia Fields' treacherous Course Number 4, this time Ferebee and Caschetta agreed to start on Course Number 1, the handi-work of former newspaper typesetter and naturalist Tom Bendelow.

Teeming with adrenaline after mending his rift with Angie and hearing the heartfelt encouragement from fellow Olympia Fields members, Ferebee attended a quick luncheon in his honor and started across the par-75 at 1:20 p.m. Initially, he offered almost no hint that his right leg was seriously injured.

He hoofed around Number 1 in an hour and 22 minutes, shooting an unin-spired score of 17-over-par 89 before turning his attention to Willie Park's awe-some Number 4. Finding some rhythm with his putter, Ferebee gradually tore into the 6,900-yard beast.

After making bogey on all but one hole on the front side to finish at 8-over 43, Ferebee rattled off pars on holes 10 through 12. Twice he holed long putts to save par, thrilling a growing audience. Folks had completed their free rounds and stayed to watch Ferebee.

However, the momentum faded just as quickly as it came. Ferebee played the final six holes in 5 over par to finish the back side with 40 strokes and an ag-gregate score of 13-over-par 83. Still, under any circumstances it was a remarkable score on one of the country's toughest courses. As he ambled over to the first tee of Course Number 2 the gallery applauded Ferebee as if he were one of the greats of his day, Sam Snead or Ben Hogan.

Ferebee never understood why so many Olympia Fields members thought Number 2 was such easy pickings. Yes, the course was relatively short at 6,330 yards. Yes, it was almost completely flat, with easy access from one green to the next tee. And it was true that Number 2 had fewer trees and less interference from Butterfield Creek than its other three counterparts did.

But Ferebee had never come close to challenging its par of 72. With the pain seeping back into his right leg after Dr. Alexander decided to loosen the bandage, his play wasn't going to be any different this day.

The best score he posted on the first 9 was a par 4 on the opening hole, a mere 230 yards long. The other eight holes were an awkward jumble of bogeys and higher, and he made the turn at 10-over-par 46.

Again, he pounced on the back nine. He birdied the par-3 10th after his tee shot landed six feet from the flag and held. He bent his tee shot perfectly around the big bend to the right on the 11th to set up a par 4. He made par 4 at 12, a straight-ahead 302 yards. He slipped at 13 with a bogey 5, but he rebounded on the 295-yard 14th with another par.

For the first time in three days, and despite pain that sapped much of the spring from his step, Ferebee suddenly enjoyed playing golf again. Most of his tee shots found the fairway or relatively harmless areas of rough. He, Caschetta, and the forecaddies who had served him so well the previous month were in sync. The right club was waiting for him when he arrived. Yardages were being calibrated quickly and accurately. From tee to green, Ferebee's swing was grooved, though his pace was labored.

Still, there was no beating the curse of the ordinary golfer, which states that when the swing is working, the putter is not, or vice versa. Ferebee kept hitting the ball solidly and straight, but his touch with the putter withered away to nothing. He played the last four holes in 3 over par, for an 18-hole tally of 85.

It was beginning to get dark when Ferebee started Number 3. A par-70 Bendelow-Watson collaboration, most members hated the course the moment they laid eyes on it.

With the pain in his leg reducing his gait now to a hobble and a poorly camouflaged grimace crossing his face with each lunge at the ball, Ferebee fashioned his best scores on the six holes that statistically were easiest. The other 12, however, were a royal struggle, particularly the final three.

Lighting the way from behind him was South Chicago's floodlight fire truck. Just its presence rekindled horrible flashbacks of the previous night's fall in St. Louis. Although Ferebee knew the ups and downs of Olympia Fields' Number 3 as well as he knew the way around his home, he and Caschetta proceeded so cautiously that it took two hours and 42 minutes to complete the course in 19-over-par 89.

Ferebee was ashamed, but the crowd, several thousand strong, didn't care about Ferebee's scores or the time it took to shoot them. They had taken great pride in shepherding him down one fairway to the next, shouting encouragement, offering him food and drink (on Alexander's orders, he declined), and cheering loudly for even the most mediocre results.

It was practically midnight at the Sharp Stick. The Tall Man and his eight bettors had just gotten word that Ferebee had finished in Chicago.

"If anyone wants out, now's the time to say so," The Tall Man said. "You'll walk out of here with $300, not bad for a couple of days of doing nothing."

No one spoke. The Tall Man waited patiently.

"Okay," he finally said. "You're all in. Hey, by this time tomorrow, you guys could be splitting more than six grand!"

After the eight men had dispersed into a wet, dreary night, The Tall Man dialed Chicago.

"This Ferebee's quite a guy," he began pleasantly. "Is he going to make it? . . . No way? . . . He's that bad off? I don't buy it. The papers here say he just keeps going like nothing . . . Okay, I believe you. . . Hope you're right."

As he was saying good-bye, one of the newer girls on the street walked in, seeking shelter from the heavy rain outside. Business was terrible, driven off by the storm. Would The Tall Man like some company for the rest of the night? He'd done her so many favors.

"Another time," he replied, ushering her back outside so he could lock up. "I'm meeting someone first thing in the morning on the other side of town, and I need some rest."

Adolph Goodwin had tracked Ferebee step for step across Olympia Fields. He didn't know what to make of the golfer's physical condition. Sometimes, his stride appeared almost normal. At other times, it was painfully obvious to everyone that Ferebee's right leg couldn't possibly allow him to cover another 40 or so miles on foot.

But Ferebee had made a habit of proving his detractors wrong. The man's stamina and will were unlike anything Goodwin had ever seen.

That observation is exactly what Goodwin told Jack Reilly when he phoned the World's Fair director of special events in New York. Using the phone from the end of the clubhouse opposite the men's showers and away from the crowd waiting for Ferebee, he enthused, "Jack, he's putting on a hell of show, just like I told you he would. I hope you're ready, because J. Smith Ferebee is on his way!"

Chicago: 72 holes—89-83-85-89-346

9

A Dangerous Fog in Philadelphia

The delay in reaching Milwaukee had been inevitable considering Ferebee's nasty fall and resulting injury in St. Louis and the fact that the Milwaukee airport was closed. No one was to blame, though some people on board the *TRANE of the Air* still chafed over the time they had forfeited when Ferebee decided to dine at Norwood Hills. But now the news Captain Bowe had received from the airport in Camden, New Jersey, presented an altogether different problem. The runway at Central Camden Airport, 40 minutes from North Hills Country Club outside Philadelphia, was too short to accommodate the DC-3. They had one alternative: Fly to Newark, charter a smaller plane, and fly back to Camden. It was an inconvenience that no one on board the *TRANE of the Air* needed.

"Goodwin's damn lucky he's not here right now!" Trane screeched after Bowe filled him in on the latest setback. "How could he have not known this? What was he thinking?"

Bowe headed for Newark, the busiest airport in the world. Just behind him in the Honeymoon Hut, Ferebee rolled his bloodshot eyes. It had only been a few hours since the festive stop in Chicago, but judging from the way he felt, he might as well have been there a month ago. The relentless pain in his right leg and the near-continuous turbulence experienced at 10,000 feet made it impossible for him to sleep for more than a few minutes at a time.

He looked at Angie. Snuggled in the upper sleeper, she was having no such trouble.

Officials at North Hills had graciously agreed to have someone on duty all night inside their "locker house." Whenever Ferebee arrived—estimated to be around 3 a.m.—he could sleep on one of their massage tables and thus be fresh for what would be a grueling final day.

Now those plans were worthless. Trane and Ferebee quickly designated a new travel party to join them aboard the smaller plane. Caschetta and Tuerk were obvious choices. So was Dr. Alexander, who had taken to using various treatments on Ferebee's leg in hopes of dulling the pain.

Ferebee didn't dare leave Angie behind. Al the stowaway and Snowball the dog had developed into a useful human interest angle for the press. He needed Fred Pederson, the Trane publicity man, to tend to the Philly writers.

Bowe would transport everyone else to Mitchel Field on Long Island. They would land less than a mile from the group's final stop later that day, Salisbury Golf Club.

Finding a pilot to come out in the middle of the night wasn't easy, but Trane's promise of a handsome payoff was persuasion enough for one nearby aviator.

It was 4:45 a.m. when Ferebee, Angie, Caschetta, and Pederson finally flopped into the lead car carrying the group from Central Camden to North Hills. It was a trip that Ferebee later described as "the most harrowing of my life."

Driving as though he had just picked up outlaws Bonnie and Clyde outside a bank, Ferebee's chauffeur completed the normally 40-minute trip in only 17. The mad scramble across the Benjamin Franklin Bridge and over the dimly lit and foggy streets of Glenside, Pennsylvania, plunged Ferebee into a foul mood.

A smattering of spectators watched him continuously rub a hand over his forehead as he shuffled into the locker house at North Hills. The chatty Pederson tried to boost his spirits by joking that he'd never ridden in a car before whose tires hadn't actually touched the road.

Ferebee ignored him.

"Terrible, terrible headache," Ferebee grumbled to a locker-room attendant who had made the mistake of asking how he was doing. Ferebee sent Pederson outside to find Alexander, but he was told that the car carrying the doctor, Tuerk, Trane, and the stowaway either had become separated from the group or was lost. Either way, it hadn't arrived yet.

Ferebee doused his face with water, rolled up the cuffs of his bright white slacks, and sighed as he ventured outside. Passing a long buffet table soon to be loaded with breakfast treats for Trane's reception guests, he was greeted by a half-dozen men. Looking around, he noticed that they were the only people visible anywhere on the property. He was filling a glass with his usual early morning orange juice when a man sporting a handlebar mustache approached from the other end of the table.

"My name is Tallman," the man began, offering a handshake that Ferebee gingerly accepted. "I can't tell you how impressed I am that you've made it this far. I wouldn't have thought it possible."

"Well, if my head doesn't feel better soon, this could be the end of it," Ferebee replied. "It hurts so bad that it's painful just to open my eyes. I'm already dealing with a bad shank—and I don't mean my golf."

Startled by the cracked shell of a man whose hand he had just released, Tallman momentarily diddled with the tips of his mustache before continuing. "What you're describing sounds terrible," he said, "but I may be able to help."

Tallman explained that he was a local pharmacist and had come early to watch Ferebee play a little before heading to work and opening his shop. He could identify with Ferebee's predicament. He was prone to headaches himself, torrents of pain that erupted almost without warning. For that reason, he routinely carried his own powdered pain reliever with him.

"It tastes just awful," Tallman warned, "but mixing it with juice will help."

While Ferebee began to stretch, Tallman poured him a second glass.

"I'm sure this will do the trick," he said.

Moments later, Ferebee lowered the empty glass and announced that if someone would point him to the first tee, he would get started. Caschetta was already waiting for him, offering last-minute instructions to Frank Deverant, the local caddie hired to handle the first round. Caschetta patted Ferebee on the back, then started down the first fairway.

Philadelphia at dawn was encased in a dense curtain of fog. It was chilly. The few folks on the property wore sweaters to ward off the first cool morning air of early fall. With his sweaters and jacket on the DC-3 in Newark, Ferebee had donned a long-sleeve white shirt.

Like wet mortar, a thick glaze of dew saturated North Hills. Caschetta told himself that it wouldn't take long before Ferebee's last dry pair of golf shoes became soaked. He knew what the wet leather and wool would do to his friend's blistered feet.

After several practice swings, Ferebee's first shot whizzed over Art's head, sliced through the vapor, and settled in the fairway. The forecaddies flocked to it. Caschetta clapped his hands and jogged toward the green. Despite the physical grind of the last three days, he felt strong.

Although blessed with a well-manicured layout in a pastoral setting, North Hills was not a club where every golfer took himself too seriously. A wild swinger once hooked his drive over the fence that separated the property from the railroad tracks, and the ball landed atop a passing coal car whose next stop was Bethlehem, 40 miles away. Calls were immediately placed to Robert Ripley in New York, claiming that the course should now be considered home to the world's longest drive. When Ripley declared it so in print, a party was thrown to celebrate.

From its beginning, North Hills stood apart in relishing eccentricity.

In 1907, a Germantown nurseryman named J. Franklin Meehan teamed with the chief engineer of the local parks commission to design a rough-hewn nine-hole course. Initially determined to keep the club a male-only enclave, Meehan and his cronies ruled that North Hills was off-limits to women; they wouldn't even be allowed to drive onto the property. Their wives soon convinced them of the shortsightedness of that action, and by 1938, North Hills was justifiably proud of its crackerjack women's golf team.

Those folks with an itch to gamble could scratch it at North Hills. In the early days of the Depression, when more than half the members tendered their resignation, the North Hillers knew how to draw a crowd. They converted part of their golf course into a dog track that, one publication claimed, "the sportiest gamblers flocked to." It was true, at least until the state police raided the operation. The Pennsylvania Liquor Control Board once suspended North Hills' license after discovering that the club sponsored regular weekend-long poker games and offered members and their guests access to a dozen well-worn slot machines.

Even the course itself was peculiar. Meehan eventually added a second nine holes. But he was forced to cram his design onto a mere 126 acres, parts of it interrupted by a disused iron mine. On the 10th and 11th holes, a quarry measuring 50 feet deep and100 yards wide came into play. On number 11, a player was forced to maneuver his ball through a fairway opening only 20 yards wide to a green that sat on the edge of the pit.

With the course encased in fog, only The Tall Man, the caddie Deverant, a couple of kids planning to play hooky, and two cops from the Camden Airport motorcade escorted Ferebee. Everyone else rationalized that it made no sense to watch someone play golf if they couldn't actually see anything.

Ferebee started decently enough, using 11 strokes in making bogeys on the first two holes. Then he hammered a 5-iron shot 160 yards onto the third green and two-putted for a par 3.

Although his play hadn't suffered, his headache hadn't dissipated; in fact, it was rapidly gaining strength. Ferebee felt as if someone was trapped inside his skull and was tunneling to escape. He was having trouble processing the information Deverant was attempting to relay.

At 570 yards, number 4 was the longest hole on the course. Ferebee was all over the place, using five strokes to reach the green and three putts for a triple-bogey 8.

"They'll be calling me 'Three-putt Willie' back at Chicago when they hear about this round," he muttered to Deverant, shaking his head in disgust.

Another three-putt on number 5 resulted in a double-bogey 6. On the sixth hole, he pulled his drive left and out of bounds. He laid five when he finally found the smallish green. Again, he used three putts to saddle himself with an embarrassing quadruple-bogey 8.

"That stuff you gave me isn't working," he snapped at Tallman, who suddenly appeared out of the fog and stood next to the marathoner. He had been following the play from a respectable distance behind Ferebee, figuring he could better gauge the path of the ball, among other things.

Scowling momentarily, Tallman studied the golfer. Then his mood suddenly brightened. "You sound just like all of my other customers," Tallman joked. "It's barely had a chance to work. Give it some time."

Tallman glanced around. The surrounding holes were still void of people, but the fog would soon begin to lift. He knew that Ferebee's gallery would start to grow. It was time to postion himself for a quick getaway. He wished Ferebee good luck and patted him gently on the back.

"I don't know how you are able to play under these conditions," he offered. "I can't see enough to really enjoy this. I'm going to go in for a bit. I'll catch up with you later."

With that, he turned and headed in the direction of the clubhouse. He had seen enough. Ferebee didn't stand a chance.

Ferebee recovered a bit to finish the front nine with three consecutive bogeys, but his score of 14-over-par 49 was dismal. The pain inside his head was increasing. He even felt a little dizzy. Remaining still over the ball had become all but impossible. His shots had lost distance and accuracy as a result.

Ferebee looked around for a member of the entourage. No one was there. Caschetta was off scouting the holes ahead, his progress slowed by the fog. Trane was preparing to welcome his guests. Tuerk and Alexander had arrived shortly after Ferebee teed off, but they had settled at the clubhouse buffet. Angie, dressed in a smart black pin-striped outfit with billowed sleeves that fell to the elbow and a tall toque hat that hid the damage plane travel had inflicted on her hair, chatted with Trane and Alexander. Al the Stowaway was guiding Snowball to the front parking lot for the dog's morning constitutional. Indoors, Pederson was discussing story angles with a couple of sportswriters.

Someone in the group mentioned Seabiscuit. The extraordinary little horse's victory in a $10,000 race in Havre de Grace, Maryland, the previous day had shoved the Ferebee story below the fold of most Philadelphia sports pages. That was okay, Trane joked; his money would be on Ferebee if the golfer and the horse's handlers ever decided to stage an endurance race.

On number 10, Ferebee's tee shot dropped down short of the 175 yards needed to carry the quarry, and the ball bounded to the bottom. Trying to avoid the water hazard on the left, he needed three more shots to reach the putting surface.

Deverant's advice on how to play the 20-foot putt either went unheeded or was misunderstood. Ferebee burned three more strokes. Instead of taking advantage of a hole that should have played to his strength—accuracy over distance—Ferebee stumbled to the 11th tee having just taken a triple bogey 7.

Again he collected himself, making short work of the usually tricky 135-yard hole. Burrowing his tee shot through a narrow chute and onto the green, Ferebee easily made par.

On the 12th, a par 5, Ferebee hit the type of drive expected of someone who'd never before seen North Hills. Instead of trusting Deverant's suggested line, Ferebee misplayed his shot, which landed on a hill that sloped down to a creek. Only sheer luck and wet grass kept the ball in play, not that Ferebee took advantage of the break. By the time he was finished, Deverant was scribbling a seven on the scorecard.

Tuerk and Alexander had finally left the food and moved to the course. From the moment they arrived they could tell that something was wrong with their friend. Alexander had anticipated seeing Ferebee limp from one shot to the next, expecting him to start dragging the right leg behind him the longer he played. He was more aware than anyone of Ferebee's deepening level of fatigue, especially since he had never adjusted to the pitching of the DC-3. But although Ferebee hadn't slept more than five hours, total, since leaving Los Angeles on Sunday, Alexander still didn't understand why Ferebee was struggling to put one foot in front of the other and why he was in such a daze.

Tuerk noticed something else. Even when the pain was at its most biting, Ferebee had remained lucid and alert. He'd also been unfailingly upbeat, oozing that old Virginia charm with Trane's clients and anyone who had come to watch him play. The Ferebee he saw now carried a distant, disinterested look.

As Ferebee was finishing off a double-bogey 6 on number 13, Tuerk suddenly rumbled off to look for Caschetta. He found him surveying the 17th green. The nearly 300-pound stockbroker, who stood to lose more than anyone if Ferebee completed the marathon, gulped to catch his breath. Finally, he informed Art that Ferebee's score was already hovering around 70 with five holes still to play.

Caschetta couldn't believe it. He had scouted all but the last hole of North Hills. Even a worn-down, hobbled Ferebee would find few problems scoring low enough on this course. But at the rate Ferebee must have been squandering shots, his score couldn't help but top 100. The marathon would be over. The land would be lost.

Not having witnessed the exchange between Tallman and Ferebee at the buffet table, Caschetta's mind searched for possible answers. The local caddie, Deverant—was he involved in some kind of fix? Maybe he was deliberately misreading the putts. Or giving Ferebee the wrong yardages or under-clubbing him. It wouldn't have been hard to do, not considering the foggy conditions and the isolation in which Ferebee was tackling the opening 18. Caschetta didn't want to believe it, but who knew?

At the same time, Caschetta was acutely aware of how streaky Ferebee's game could be. When he was on, he was capable of playing much better than his 15 handicap. But the rhythm could leave him at any moment. When it did, no score was too high. Caschetta wanted to ask Tuerk to describe what Ferebee was doing wrong, but he quickly remembered that Fat Fred knew as much about playing golf as Art did about playing the stock market.

"There's something else," Tuerk finally huffed. "It's the way he looks—different. He's not the same. His mind's not right. I want to win this thing, but I sure as hell don't want to win this way."

Behind the 13th green, Alexander turned the bill of his white newsboy cap to the side and took a long, close look into Ferebee's sunken eyes. "What have you eaten today?" he asked.

"Sandwich . . . sweet roll . . . I dunno."

"And to drink?"

"A little juice . . . water."

"Anything else?"

"I took something some guy, a pharmacist, gave me for this awful damned headache. But my head is worse, and I'm dizzy."

Alexander turned to Deverant. "Go see if they've got any brandy. Now!" Alexander commanded. The boy dropped Ferebee's bag and sprinted toward the clubhouse.

"I believe you've been slipped a 'Mickey [Finn],'" Alexander explained, helping Ferebee to a bench. "From the way you look, it was only a mild one, enough to make you a little squirrelly. The brandy should help."

Deverant soon returned, lugging a partially full fifth of applejack and a beer glass.

Alexander pitched the bottle after emptying it into the glass, lifted the glass to Ferebee's lips, and slowly began tilting. "Drink it down, all of it," he commanded. "Don't stop."

Ferebee suddenly lurched over to the trash can and began vomiting. "Alex?"

"I'll explain later," the doctor replied calmly. "But that's what I wanted."

As Deverant reached for the bag, Alexander saw Caschetta dashing toward them. "Hold on, kid," the doctor ordered.

Once he was told that Ferebee's score stood at 72, Caschetta took charge. He pulled more club than his boss normally would need for his tee shot to the 14th hole, a long par 3. He led him to the tee box, positioned him in line with the flag, and stepped back.

"Don't swing until I tell you to," he instructed.

"Not too long, Art," Alexander advised.

The instant Ferebee's posture appeared as anchored and steady as it was likely to get, Caschetta yelled, "Go!" Ferebee drew the club back and forth in a pendulum-like motion. Miraculously, the shot leaped from the club cleanly and soared onto the green, about 30 feet from the hole.

Caschetta then coaxed a critical two-putt par from Ferebee, who stumbled to the green. The round could be salvaged, but there was little room for the types of mistakes Ferebee had been making all morning.

Ferebee's tee shot on the par-5 15th strayed into the trees guarding the left side. The only option was to punch the ball sideways and back into the fairway. His third shot was short, and his fourth missed the elevated green. He finally topped a shot onto the putting surface, but it was so far from the cup that he needed three putts to get in the hole for an 8.

Now he'd taken 83 strokes with three holes to go.

The 16th was a 380-yard dogleg right that required a long tee shot to avoid a blind approach shot to the green. Ferebee couldn't do it. He needed two more swings and a pair of putts to secure a bogey 5.

Somehow, Ferebee summoned the strength on number 17 to pound his drive about 200 yards through another one of North Hills' narrow chutes. But his approach shot was pitifully short of the green. He chipped onto the green, then took two putts for his second consecutive bogey 5.

Ferebee came to the 18th with only six shots to spare.

The finishing hole was a challenging conclusion for even the most skilled player. A par 4 measuring 385 yards that veered sharply left to right, some members played it as a par 5. Their strategy was to be short of the green in two, rather than slam a shot toward a green that stood on the back edge of another quarry.

They knew that a solidly struck tee shot would fly parallel to the railroad tracks and settle atop a terrace in the fairway. Any attempt to cut the dogleg was as foolhardy as it was futile, for the terrace sloped gradually down to a creek. The beauty of the hole was that even the most accurately positioned tee shot still left the player about 185 yards from the green. With the locker house on the left and the quarry ready to gobble anything even slightly right of target, average players were inclined to be conservative.

Caschetta held his breath and hoped Ferebee would hit his first two shots well enough to be about 45 yards short of the green. From there, he figured, Ferebee could lob the ball high enough to keep it on the putting surface.

The plan was unfolding perfectly until Ferebee pulled his third stroke. While it landed on the putting surface, it was perched in the far left quadrant, 45 subtly breaking feet from the hole.

As Ferebee made his way onto the green, thirty or so people, many of them employees at North Hills who had arrived early, suddenly turned their attention to him. With Caschetta surveying the putt, they began shouting instructions on which direction it would break. The stillness and eerie quiet that had engulfed the course for 17 holes had suddenly given way to a confusing mishmash of noise.

While Caschetta analyzed the putt from every conceivable angle, North Hills pro Bill Neilan strode onto the green and raised his arms to demand silence. Ferebee, shaky, drew the putter back but stubbed the blade into the grass directly behind the ball. When it stopped rolling, he still had 30 feet to navigate.

Once again, advice rang out from the gallery. Neilan repeated his command for calm. Still playing to the same line, Ferebee made a much firmer pass at the ball. His 98th shot of the morning rolled and rolled, skittering to a stop 16 inches past the cup.

Caschetta took no chances, holding Ferebee back while he gave the new line a quick read. It was straight. Squatting, Caschetta pointed to the center of the cup. After settling himself with three short, smooth practice strokes, Ferebee sent the ball where Caschetta's finger had been moments before.

There was polite applause until Deverant stepped forward and announced, "Mr. Ferebee's score for the first round—99!"

The applause immediately intensified. Some cried out their approval. Angie covered her mouth with her hand and blinked back tears. Caschetta smiled for the first time since joining the group at the 14th hole. Holding Ferebee's arm as they started up an incline to the clubhouse, Alexander quietly suggested that he scan the area for the man who had given him the "headache powder."

But Ferebee recognized no one.

Standing atop a hill at the edge of the parking lot, The Tall Man had turned and walked briskly to his car the moment he heard Deverant's pronouncement at the 18th green. He was on his way back to the safety of South Philadelphia before Ferebee had handed Caschetta his putter.

Inside the clubhouse, Alexander immediately apologized to Ferebee for not having been with him from the start of the round. He chastised himself for his decision to ride with Tuerk and Trane rather than in the lead car.

He explained that chloral hydrate, the drug he suspected Ferebee had been given, slowed a person's heart rate, circulation, and respiration. A physician at a hospital would have started treatment by pumping out Ferebee's stomach. Gulping the brandy had caused a similar result and jump-started his system.

Alexander then insisted that Ferebee take an hour before heading back to the course. He helped the golfer onto the massage table, examined his throbbing leg, adjusted the bandages, and changed the dressing on his foot blisters.

Caschetta, Trane, and Tuerk joined them. When Trane heard the details, he immediately wondered whether someone in their inner circle had been involved in trying to spoil the bet. He kept wondering about that morning's travel snafu, one he maintained Goodwin should easily have been able to avoid. Could the ad executive have had a role in this scheme?

Caschetta had questioned Deverant outside the locker house and had asked when he had been assigned to carry Ferebee's clubs. Deverant assured him that he hadn't been told until he arrived at the club that morning. Even if he'd wanted to, he had not had the time to devise a plan for Ferebee to fail.

Tuerk went back outside and found a couple of people he'd spotted earlier at the buffet table. Did anyone recognize the man Ferebee had been talking to right before he teed off? No one had ever seen him before; in fact, when they saw him walk behind Ferebee to the first tee, they'd assumed that he belonged with the traveling party.

Frustrated, Tuerk returned inside. The bottom line, all reluctantly agreed, was that they had neither the time nor the means to find out whether anyone else was involved. They wouldn't see Goodwin until the marathon was over, and they had absolutely no evidence to implicate him. They'd have to live with their suspicions.

By the end of the hour, Ferebee's condition had improved greatly. Although still slightly dazed, he returned to the course and began playing more the way Caschetta had anticipated. North Hills was drying out and the fog had all but given way. Ferebee posted a second-round score of 85, or 14 strokes lower than the first round.

With Trane's reception over and a gallery of about 300 people tracking Ferebee shot for shot on the third round, he posted a near–carbon copy 85 that included six pars on the front nine.

He completed the fourth and final round with a 16-over-par 87, but he saved his most memorable shots for last. After blasting a perfect drive on number

18, Ferebee not only avoided the quarry with his 4-wood approach shot, but his ball stopped 15 feet from the hole.

When he tapped in for par moments later, he had completed 72 holes in six hours, 14 minutes. This time, the ovation was lengthy and loud enough to be heard down the street in Edge Hill.

"Are you sick of it all by now?" he was asked as he entered the locker house to shower and change clothes.

"And how. If only I could stay right here."

Philadelphia: 72 holes—99-85-85-87-356

10

A Ghostly Trail

Ferebee was still three days and a couple of thousand miles from arriving in New York when Jack Reilly issued a memo to 1939 World's Fair president Grover Whalen, assistant Howard A. Flanigan, and the chairmen of seven committees. Director of Special Events Reilly briefly outlined Ferebee's "race across the country in a plane." Apparently not a golfer, he informed his colleagues of the plan to bring Ferebee to the fairgrounds "where he will sink his final put [*sic*]."

"The way this stunt is building up publicity," he wrote, "it is quite possible that the sinking of the final put [*sic*] will be covered by newsreel and camera men. . . . Be prepared for an emergency."

Reilly had no idea how many emergencies everyone connected to Ferebee would have to deal with on September 28. The golfer's apparent drugging and near-disastrous 99 at North Hills that morning were only the beginning.

Practically everyone was scrambling. Capt. Ed Bowe radioed Mitchel Field on Long Island that he would land the DC-3 as scheduled but without Ferebee and the other prominent members of the party. They were still on the golf course in Philadelphia, where the itinerary was in tatters.

That change meant someone at Mitchel Field or on the DC-3 was saddled with explaining the delay to the dozens of reporters, photographers, and newsreel cameramen who were waiting impatiently for their story of the day to arrive. A hasty order was placed to the mess hall for someone to set up a table inside one of the smaller hangars and stock it with sandwiches and cold beer. Everyone knew that the only thing the press liked more than a story that wrote itself was a free meal.

It worked, at least temporarily. The newshounds chomped and chugged placidly while rooting around the DC-3, killing time chatting with Bowe and, especially, stewardess Lillian Fette.

But there was a limit to how long even a woman of Fette's considerable poise and charm could keep reporters at bay. No one was happier than American Airlines' first star in a skirt when word came that the small plane carrying Ferebee and the rest of the party finally landed at about 1:30 p.m., or ninety minutes late.

The golfing wizard was herded over to a bank of microphones set up only a few feet from the DC-3. He briefly answered some questions, but it was clear that he was hardly in a mood to talk.

"Listen, fellas, I still have a lot of work to do before this thing is over," he finally interjected. "Let's pick this up later." With that, Ferebee, Trane, and the entire team—Bowe and Fette, too—headed for the finish line.

Less than a mile away, Salisbury Golf Links pro Pete Cassella faced an unexpected dilemma—night golf. Ferebee had been slated to finish his final 72 holes around the dinner hour. Now the 28-year-old club professional found himself desperately searching for some method of illuminating his golf course.

He wasn't only concerned with Ferebee's well-being. Hundreds of people who'd never before set foot on Salisbury needed to see where they were going.

Ferebee arrived at Salisbury's Course Number 4—today known as Eisenhower Park–Red Course—at exactly 1:53 p.m. He was more than a little curious about what he would find. The course had a solid reputation, having been designed for New York's posh set in 1914 by Devereux Emmet, a man more than a little familiar with a lifestyle of privilege.

He was descended from Thomas Addison Emmet, one of the founders of Tammany Hall. His father-in-law was Alexander Turney Stewart, an Irish immigrant who had made millions in the dry goods business and established the neighboring village of Garden City. Having been around such extravagant amounts of money all of his life, Devereux Emmet viewed it with such nonchalance that he actually designed his first couple of golf courses for free.

Emmet's two great passions were hunting and golf. He excelled at both, having once advanced to the quarterfinals of the British Amateur championship. Meanwhile, all who knew of them prized the hunting dogs he trained. Ultimately, Emmet managed to meld the two pastimes into a unique and highly profitable existence. He trained hunting dogs in America in spring and summer, sold them in Ireland in autumn, and spent winters hunting and golfing in the British Isles. There, he was introduced to the design superstar of his age, C. B. Macdonald, who invited Emmet's help on designing his homage to the revered courses of Scotland, the National Golf Links of America in Southampton, New York. From that point on, Emmet was hooked.

Parading around dusty job sites wearing a three-piece white suit and white shoes, with a pipe peering out over the breast pocket of his coat, Emmet built dozens of courses before his death in 1934. Working during the era of hickory-shafted clubs, Emmet created courses that rarely measured more than 6,300 yards but never lacked for difficulty.

His Course Number 4 at Salisbury was no exception. The Professional Golf Association of America considered it formidable enough to host its 1926 championship. Dapper Walter Hagen exhibited all of his wondrous talent and rascally charm that week before finally routing Leo Diegel, 5 and 3, in the match play final.

Judging from the chitchat Salisbury pro Pete Cassella overheard from the small gallery waiting at the course for Ferebee, the people were expecting to see a stylish amateur cut from the Hagen mold. It was understandable. Few, if any, photos had accompanied the newspaper stories they'd read of Ferebee's earlier rounds that week. Those photos that were published in New York usually had shown Ferebee smiling, waving, and mugging for photographers while cradling Snowball.

While wire service reporters noted Ferebee's injured leg in all of their transmissions, no one had confirmed the severity of his condition. Besides, only someone who was in healthy condition could play as much golf in as little time as Ferebee had these last three days.

Meanwhile, although his appearance had improved greatly since leaving Philadelphia, it could hardly be qualified as debonair, flamboyant, or suave. The effects of the Mickey Finn were gone, as was his headache, but the lack of sleep had forced Ferebee's eyes to retreat deep into their sockets. In place of the once sparkling, sleek, and carefree dandy the crowd was expecting stood a gaunt specter. Down 20 pounds since Sunday, he had taken a knife from the galley of the DC-3 that morning and burrowed a hole in his belt in order to keep his pants from falling down.

Dr. Alexander had covered the blisters on both of Ferebee's hands with ointment-saturated gauze that he only removed when they landed on Long Island. The blisters on his feet he'd treated with more Cur-A-Ped cream and pads. Alexander had also tucked Ferebee's right leg into a tight and intricate quilt of bandages that ran from his inner thigh to his ankle. Now Ferebee dragged it behind him as if he were a mule pulling a plow, shedding all pretense of agility.

Despite it all and guided by a superb local caddie, Ferebee thrilled the gallery by opening with an adrenaline-powered 85 that took a mere 92 minutes. Almost two hours to the minute later, he ended his second trip around Number 4 with a score of 92. It was 5:27 p.m.

The setting sun had ushered in a chilly dampness that seeped inside a person's bones and made even teetotalers crave a drink that was a wee bit stronger. As Ferebee began his third round, the nearby Westbury Fire Department was driving over a fire truck with two searchlights mounted behind the open-air front seat. Pete Cassella's frantic prayer for light had been answered.

The gallery continued to grow. Many of the newcomers had stopped at the course on their way home from work, figuring they'd catch the final few holes. They were surprised not only by how much golf Ferebee still had to play but also by his inartistic performance.

Guided by the Westbury Fire Department's lights for the final nine holes, Ferebee closed out the third round with scores of 7, 7, 5, 7, and 5. At 7:24 p.m. he signed a scorecard that read 91.

Instead of returning to the first tee for his final 18, Ferebee whispered to Alexander that he desperately needed a break. Five hours and 31 minutes had elapsed since he'd hit the first shot at Salisbury, or more time than he'd needed to complete 72 holes or more at his other stops.

A few days earlier, Ferebee had envisioned blazing around this final course at the same electrifying pace he'd displayed in Los Angeles. Now, he thought, he'd be lucky if he could crawl across the finish line.

Inside the casino that sat near the first tee, Ferebee slipped off his slacks to show Alexander an ugly rash that was popping out from the top of the bandage on his right leg. Wrapping the leg tightly had fortified his ankle and knee and kept the pain to a minimum. It had also been effective because the bizarre truth was that Ferebee hobbled as fast as most people jogged. But either the friction from the bandage or maybe the adhesive that held it in place created a rash that had grown worse since it appeared in Chicago the day before. When Alexander stripped the bandage off to apply an ointment, a searing pain thundered down Ferebee's leg.

"What would people say if I just walked out of here right now?" Ferebee mused.

"They'd say you were even more of a wack than they took you for at the start of this thing," Alexander replied. "They'd insist you see a head doctor, and they'd want his report put on the front page."

Alexander paused, allowing his mind to wander to the public tempest Ferebee would create if he just walked away after expending all of this time, energy, and money. How would the rest of his loyal entourage feel about such a betrayal of trust? Alexander had never been one for self-pity.

"Then again, Smitty, life would go on," the doctor continued, his sarcasm and irritation obvious. "In case you haven't heard, Hitler's kicking down some doors in Europe, and he's got Benito Mussolini with him. No one gives a damn about your little farm in Virginia. It's been a nice little diversion for everybody, but can we please get the hell back out there, finish it, and go home?"

Ferebee stared back, amused. "I see you've had time to read the papers," he quipped. "Lillian's a nurse, right? Hell, call her in here. The way you are right now, I'm not sure I want you wrapping my leg."

Alexander's anger calmed.

"If Angie sees Lillian come in here, you're gonna need a lot more than your leg wrapped," he teased. "Believe me, you're better off with me."

His leg finally retaped, Ferebee began the last round at 7:45 p.m. In order to keep the Virginia plantation and force Tuerk to pay the mortgage, he had barely four hours to walk another 18 holes and shoot less than 100.

The chill around him had deepened. The course seemed to be suffocating in a heavy mist, forcing Ferebee to don a jacket over his white, long-sleeved shirt. He tugged the collar up.

The crowd had swelled to more than 500 people, many of them shivering. The guys on the fire truck sipped coffee and fidgeted. What would happen if they were needed elsewhere?

Back at Chicago's Olympia Fields, members and caddies shared benches inside the massive men's locker room in a rare display of social equality. "Putter" Corrado, the caddie clerk who had accompanied Ferebee for 90 holes in August, brought a chalkboard into the locker room. Across the top, he printed "Salisbury, Sept. 28." Beneath it, he wrote the numerals from one to 18 in three rows across, six to a column.

The wire services planned to provide brief updates after the first nine holes of the final 18, then every three holes until the finish. One of Olympia Fields' complimentary press members from the *Chicago Evening American* arranged for a copyboy to phone the locker room and relay the unfolding details as soon as he tore it from the machine.

The wait would be uncomfortably long. Ferebee's maneuvering through the Salisbury course was slow, workmanlike, and void of athletic spirit. His shots landed and stopped almost immediately whenever he missed the fairway by a couple of feet. When he most needed a friendly roll to bleed every yard from every shot, he received none.

Behind him, the firemen working the searchlights weren't accustomed to following a small, darting object like a golf ball. They'd track it briefly as it took flight, usually long enough for someone in the crowd to catch the general direction in which it was headed. This system worked well enough for shots that landed in the fairway or on the green, but Ferebee's strokes were increasingly short and off-line.

Soon, additional forecaddies were drafted from the gallery. Then Trane sent one of the groundskeepers to buy $100 worth of railroad flares. The red ones were distributed among the forecaddies with instructions to embed three of them on each side of the fairway when Ferebee reached the tee. When the firemen tilted their searchlights into the clouds, it was the signal to ignite the flares so Ferebee had somewhere to aim.

More than 75 minutes after Ferebee started the final 18, the kid from the wire room finally phoned Olympia Fields. The crowded locker room hushed as Corrado hung up and grabbed a piece of chalk. When he stepped back, the board contained nine depressingly high numbers:

7, 4, 8, 6, 5, 6, 6, 5, 6—53

1-7	2-4	3-8
4-6	5-5	6-6
7-6	8-5	9-6

Fifty-three strokes.

A collective groan arose among Fabulous Ferebee's friends and fans. Fifty-three strokes? Others, hoping at last to take some money out of Ferebee's pocket and knock him down a peg or two, rejoiced, albeit quietly.

From behind the bar at the Sharp Stick, The Tall Man was in frequent contact with the *Daily Tribune*'s switchboard in Chicago, which again was swamped with calls. He was encouraged by Ferebee's score. Despite botching the job at North Hills, The Tall Man figured that maybe he wasn't dead yet.

With nine holes to play, Ferebee's job was obvious: he needed a score of 46 or lower in order to win. It was no small feat. He had walked or run more than 175 miles in 3 ½ days. He had just hobbled up the ninth fairway while leaning on Caschetta and one of the local caddies for support, staying within the rules by keeping both feet on the ground.

Pete Cassella found Trane behind the ninth green, agonizing over Smitty's condition. Trane never before had seen an athlete exhibit the determination and grit Ferebee had displayed since Sunday, but enough was enough. Momentarily, he considered encouraging Ferebee to pack it in.

Cassella quickly erased that notion. He had a much different plan. He proposed taking over as Ferebee's strategist on the final nine holes. As the club's pro, he was certain that his knowledge of the course would save Ferebee several strokes that might prove pivotal.

Caschetta would continue to carry the bag because it was obvious to Cassella that Ferebee needed to have the kid near him. When Ferebee took his stance and said he was ready, Cassella wanted Dr. Alexander, standing behind the golfer, to light a minute flare. The additional glow would give Ferebee a better look at the ball and maybe help improve his contact.

"So now I've got *two* Italian angels?" Ferebee joked weakly when informed of the new arrangement. "Catholic boys, right? Do you really think this'll work? In case you're wondering, I'm not a member of the club."

Cassella was all business. He instructed Ferebee to hit his drive just left of the fairway bunker on number 10, which would leave a clear angle for his approach shot to the green. Ferebee did as he was told, and although he used three putts from 30 feet for a bogey 5, he had escaped one of the tougher holes on the course with a minimum of trouble.

Under normal circumstances, the 11th hole would have been a definite birdie opportunity for Ferebee. Wide open and barely 275 yards long, it was Emmet's gift to players after the presumed trouble they'd have solving the 10th green. Ferebee wasn't up to making birdie, but he had surprisingly little trouble scoring a par 4.

Emmett continued his generosity on number 12, a par 5 barely more than 400 yards long. Ferebee missed the green with his second shot, but he chipped on and two-putted for another par.

At Olympia Fields, a small cheer went up when Corrado posted Ferebee's next scores:

10-5   11-4   12-5

The par-3 13th featured a huge green. Emmet had compensated for the 200-yard tee shot that was required before any putting could be done. Ferebee came up short and pitched on, but he took three putts from 35 feet for a double-bogey 5.

He followed that with a bogey 5 on number 14. The score left him with four holes to play in only 22 strokes.

The 15th required a long, accurate tee shot in order to have any chance at birdie or par. Ferebee's drive traveled about 200 yards, and what should have been a relatively simple approach landed in the bunker guarding the right side of the green.

Gouging the ball out of wet sand and onto a green that sloped away from him, Ferebee did well to stop his blast 20 feet past the hole. Nonetheless, three putts later, he walked off with a double-bogey 6.

In Chicago, Corrado posted the latest update on the chalkboard:

13-5   14-5   15-6

Cries of "Attaboy, Smitty," "Goddamn, Ferebee," and, "He'll make it now!" rang out in Olympia Fields' locker room.

Hundreds of miles away, pro Pete Cassella wasn't so sure. Ferebee still had three holes to play. Included was the par-5 17th, which featured a blind bunker and some of the most punitive rough on the course. Then there was number 18, a long par 4 rated the second-hardest hole on the course. He'd seen plenty of members make triple bogey or higher there.

With the end in sight, Ferebee was hitting the ball better than Cassella would have imagined. But he would need to continue to play that way; Ferebee had squandered a lot of strokes on the front side.

Additionally, just getting around the course was becoming more of an adventure—and more dangerous—by the minute. The firemen were still working the searchlights, but Alexander's luck with the minute flares was erratic, at best. Some lit; more didn't. The air over Salisbury was so moist that many of the flares turned into duds.

The whole tedious, inexact exercise was immensely frustrating—and comical. Ferebee would hedge back and forth over the ball until Alexander found a flare dry enough to provide more than a momentary illumination.

They arrived at the tee of number 16. A par 3 measuring a mere 136 yards and featuring a large green, it gave the appearance of being another one of Emmet's "gift" holes. In fact, although it was considered the easiest hole on the course, it was well bunkered, and the green featured steep, sweeping slopes that placed a premium on accuracy.

Using a 6 iron to cut through the heavy night air, Ferebee landed his shot 12 feet from the cup. After a small hop, the ball teetered on the crest of a slope, only a revolution or two from a downhill roll that would have left a much longer, trickier putt. But it stopped.

Buoyed by his good fortune, he finished the hole with two putts for a 3. It was only his second par on the back nine.

At the 460-yard 17th hole, Ferebee was woefully short but down the middle with his drive. His second stroke avoided danger but was short enough to leave him with about a 100-yard pitch to a green about half the size of the one he'd just finished.

His third shot missed the green and nestled deep into the grass. It remained there after his fourth stroke. His fifth rocketed out low and hot and scurried to the far edge of the putting surface.

With at least 30 feet to negotiate and determined not to be short, Ferebee started the ball to the hole and immediately got the sick feeling that he'd struck it too forcefully. But the ball quickly lost steam. Instead of rolling past the cup, it finished 10 feet shy of the target.

Ferebee had lapsed into one of his most common mistakes. While he was a solid putter, he occasionally lined up with his eyes behind the ball instead of directly over top of it. That position caused the putter to be slightly closed when it struck the ball. Not only did that throw putts off-line, it took away distance.

Caschetta recognized what was happening and reminded Ferebee to check his posture before making his next stroke. The putt broke ever so slightly from left to right and wasn't difficult to make, if he could be confident that he was starting the ball on the right line.

Ferebee addressed the ball and double-checked to make sure he was staring directly down at its Gold Crown logo. Everything was right. He drew back the putter, followed through, and watched as the ball dived into the hole.

The gallery hooted its approval. Ferebee whirled and slapped Caschetta on the back. The kid who always seemed to be around when the best things happened to Ferebee had been there again.

About 400 yards long, much of it a steady climb uphill, the 18th possessed all the trappings of a true championship finish. Emmet had placed bunkers and gnarly rough on both sides of a narrow fairway. Ferebee had little room to stray.

The searchlights found the clouds. The fairway flares were lit. Ferebee swung his driver for the last time and sent the ball floating toward the light. It landed on the right side of the fairway, with one of the forecaddies waving a white towel and placing it atop the ball before leaving to join his buddies on the green.

Lester Rice of the *New York Journal-American* observed the scene from the back of the fire truck, furiously scribbling a story that his dictation desk would soon hear: "No hooded meeting of the Ku Klux Klan ever was more weird. Ghostly figures, hundreds of them, trailed in the wake of a grim-faced man who haltingly dragged one foot after another, his shoulders rising at every pain-racked step to ease the torture of feet blistered and swollen."

Now only 170 yards from the green, Ferebee again aimed for the flares ahead but missed short and to the right. Under a crescent moon and surrounded by businessmen in suits, Ferebee took a 2 iron from Pete Cassella and followed his advice to hit a low pitch and roll.

The ball hopped onto the green and headed for the flag. As it rolled closer to the cup and began to slow, the gallery suddenly raised its voice in a mass of anticipation. The shot was going to hit the flagstick. It might even fall into the hole. At the last instant, however, it veered just enough to roll over the edge of the hole without grazing the pin. By the time it had stopped, the ball was five feet past the target.

The gallery offered a momentary groan. Then, recognizing the brilliance of the stroke, 500 people broke into a frenzy of appreciative cheering.

Many who had taken shelter from the cold now surrounded the green, some carrying flashlights. Other spectators held lighters. Some pulled out matches.

Caschetta handed Ferebee his Calamity Jane putter, whispered that he'd never face an easier putt in his life, and stepped back. He turned to the gallery and raised his hand, their signal to train their light on the withered figure in the dusty, now cream-colored slacks.

Standing behind Ferebee, Alexander lit another flare. The firemen trained their rapidly dimming lights on the green. Cassella said a silent prayer that there wouldn't be a sudden blackout.

At precisely 10:30 p.m., Ferebee made a pass at the ball that was uncommonly smooth and athletic for someone in such wretched physical condition.

Even before the ball tumbled out of sight, the crowd started forward to embrace him. Some tossed their hats into the late-night sky. Snowball barked at the onrushing gang and strained at the leash.

Angie ran to him. In an uncharacteristic display of affection, she hugged her husband tightly and kissed his cheek. Alexander and Caschetta were right behind her. Off to the side, Trane and Tuerk shook hands, with Tuerk grinning broadly as he congratulated the industrialist. They watched Ferebee for a moment and then, side by side, hurried to the clubhouse. They would wait for him there.

Moments later inside Olympia Fields, Corrado posted the final three scores and circled the total, 96. Already giddy over the Cubs' 6-5 victory over Pittsburgh that vaulted them over the Pirates and into first place that afternoon, the locker room erupted in a second celebration.

Ferebee's friends pranced around the room, waving towels, slapping backs, shaking hands, shouting out toasts, and chugging beer. In some corners of the room, men began a mostly good-natured exchange of cash and IOUs.

In Philadelphia, The Tall Man placed one last call to Chicago. As he stood in the side room, he nodded and gingerly replaced the telephone receiver.

"Go ahead and gloat. You won't hear me moaning," he assured the eight remaining syndicate representatives, who suddenly had more than $6,000 to divide with their investors. "That guy beat me; hell, he beat all the bookies. Who in their right mind would think anyone could do what he did?"

The Tall Man told the eight to come back in the morning to collect their shares of the money. No one dared to even suggest that he might run out on them.

"Thanks to Mister Ferebee, I know where I'll be the next few years," The Tall Man said wistfully, pointing to the bar area on the other side of the wall. "Not that he'll ever find this joint, but if he does walk in here, he'll drink all night for free. Or maybe you freeloaders can pony up a round or two. hell, what am I saying?"

Then The Tall Man paused and winked.

"If he did come, here's a bet I guarantee I wouldn't lose: he'd be drunker than a couple of sailors on shore leave when he left, and there'd be something sweet on his arm to rock him to sleep."

Off the 18th green, a car arrived to take Ferebee to the clubhouse. Caschetta and Cassella—his Italian angels—hopped in and guided him up the stairs and into the locker room for a quick shower. He still had a 30-minute drive to the World's Fair grounds and one more swing to go.

Several hundred guests of Fiorello LaGuardia's awaited Ferebee's arrival in front of the Administration Building. The portly mayor grabbed his hand and led the city's newest sports hero over to the crowd and a flat area where a makeshift green had been erected.

Caschetta handed him the putter. Ferebee looked briefly at a three-foot putt. Then he drew a loud ovation from the crowd when he knocked it into the hole.

LaGuardia laughed and clapped excitedly. When the crowd quieted, he stood in front of a mike and asked Ferebee about his future.

"It won't be long before we go back to Chicago," the golfer replied quietly. "I want to get back to Olympia Fields in time for my usual 36 holes on the weekend."

Thinking that he surely was joking, the audience laughed heartily, then applauded. Perhaps realizing the absurdity of what he'd just said, Ferebee laughed, too, although he turned out to be completely serious.

Nonetheless, he had a far more immediate concern. Long after midnight, Ferebee and Angie stood at the entrance to their room at the luxurious Waldorf-Astoria Hotel on Park Avenue. Wanting to drop off his things before he headed out for a night on the town, Tuerk walked past. He handed his friend a folded cardboard sign that he had made that morning.

Ferebee opened it, laughed, and shook Tuerk's hand. As the door to their suite swung shut, Ferebee slipped the makeshift sign over the doorknob:

DON'T DISTURB 'TIL XMAS.

New York: 72 holes—85-92-91-96-364

11

Closing the Books

Ferebee and the group remained in New York for only one day before they hopped back on the DC-3 with Ed Bowe and Lillian Fette and returned to Chicago.

It was just as well. While Columbia University grad school alum Tuerk put his knowledge of New York City to good use and escorted the others on a whirl-wind tour that included Toots Shor's, Broadway, Times Square, and the Statue of Liberty, Ferebee slept in his room at the Waldorf-Astoria.

When the plane landed in Chicago on Friday the 30th, Ferebee instructed Caschetta to be ready to go 54 holes at Olympia Fields on Sunday.

"That's when I put my foot down," Caschetta recalled. "I told him, 'No way, not yet. You wanna play 18, fine. You wanna kill yourself, take someone else with you.'"

They did play 18. Afterward, Caschetta shooed Ferebee out the door.

"Hell," Caschetta said, "the man's blisters had blisters!"

As had been the case immediately after the 144-hole marathon, Ferebee was again the toast of the nation. Just the raw statistics from the golf-a-thon made it so: He played more than 33 rounds of golf in just 96 hours. He hit 2,858 shots, posting an average score of 85.7 per round, and did not lose a ball.

By his own estimate, he also went through 40 pairs of socks, eight pairs of pants, seven pair of shoes, eight golf gloves, and 48 forecaddies.

He covered 182 miles on foot and lost 21 pounds in four days; he returned to Chicago weighing 139 pounds.

It was, wrote Joseph M. Sheehan of the *New York Times*, "the most fantastic golf story ever told—or dreamed."

The *New York Journal* called Ferebee "the Hercules of Golf."

Sportswriter Bob Brumby, who had walked the Salisbury links step for step with Ferebee, opined that the golfer had waged "an amazing iron-man battle against heavy odds."

The *Los Angeles Evening Herald* screamed its approval: "J. SMITH FEREBEE, KING OF MARATHON GOLFERS!"

"FEREBEE A GRAND FELLOW, SENTIMENT THROUGHOUT U.S.," headlined one Wisconsin daily.

"When it was over," Caschetta recalled, "he told me, 'Art, I just opened the door to anywhere I want to go in the United States.' I guess he was right because for a while, everyone wanted to be seen with Smitty. He could go anywhere and do anything."

Less than a month later, Ferebee was back in New York, on stage at the Maxine Elliott Theatre for the radio program *We the People*. He mesmerized a live audience for almost 30 minutes by retelling his story, which was scripted with help from one of the show's writers.

"We want to take this opportunity to thank you for the splendid performance you gave," Robert Reuschle of *We the People* wrote to Ferebee on October 17, six days after the performance. "You may be interested to know that we received many favorable comments on your particular act from people who heard the program."

After the marathon, Ferebee approached the game more seriously. He took lessons. He practiced more often. His fame enabled him to play with top professionals Babe Didrikson, Patty Berg, and Tommy Armour. He developed some of their stroke-saving techniques. Before long, he was playing to a 3 handicap and challenging his old friend Adam Riffel—unsuccessfully, it turned out—for the club championship at Olympia Fields.

"I broke par just twice at Olympia Fields," Ferebee said in 1986. "One Sunday, I shot 68 on the Number Four Course then came back later in the day and shot 67 on the same course. I'll never forget the date: December 7, 1941."

Despite the notoriety Ferebee achieved, some people questioned whether the marathon was worth the extraordinary expense and effort.

Ferebee returned to Barney Johnson and Company. The Trane Company's sales and profits continued to grow, but there is no evidence to suggest that the marathon contributed to that. While the trip generated reams of publicity, Ferebee kept a letter from an aunt of his who gently argued that the 144-hole event received more exposure.

"I don't know for sure because I wasn't in on everything they were trying to accomplish," Caschetta said, "but I always got the impression that it didn't turn out quite the way they'd planned."

While vacationing in Winona, Minnesota, a week after the marathon, Ferebee received a letter from Reuben Trane. The climate control industrialist wrote that he hoped that Ferebee felt "as happy about the whole thing as I do. . . . It was unanimously agreed that the thing was a success for the Trane Company. Of course, it would have been an almighty flop if it hadn't been for you and your indomitable spirit to carry on to the finish. All I can say at this time is that I thank you from the bottom of my heart."

Ferebee's reply didn't quite match Trane's enthusiasm. "Although we may have wished for a somewhat different ending," he wrote without specifics, "no one can say that we did not complete what we set out to do. It is my humble opinion that there is a great deal of good and favorable publicity the Trane Company received from the affair."

Ferebee spent years being upset at the newspapers' portrayal of him as a soldier of fortune. He was accused of having a deal with Gold Crown golf balls, Fox DeLuxe beer, and the companies that manufactured his clubs, shoes, and even his clothing.

After the screen test in Los Angeles, it was reported that he craved a movie deal and would leave his job in Chicago for Hollywood as soon as the marathon was complete. Reporters also accused him of fabricating the amount of money that had been wagered. Some even said that the bet wasn't really a bet, but a ruse to nudge the Trane Company closer to the spotlight.

Most of the accusations were unfounded. Caschetta remembers going to Walgreen's the night before the train left Chicago for Los Angeles and buying the Gold Crown balls Ferebee used. Fox DeLuxe Brewery never hid the fact that it had engineered a brief promotional agreement with Ferebee following his 144-hole marathon in August. There is no evidence that he had a clothing sponsor, and Caschetta insists that Ferebee played with the same clubs he'd been using at Olympia Fields.

On the first anniversary of the marathon, Ferebee bemoaned his treatment by the press to James Kearns of the *Chicago Daily News*, who had accused Ferebee of trying to "cash in" during the marathon. Without naming names, Ferebee blamed unscrupulous "publicity" people.

"Looking back, I'll admit it was all a little crazy," he said. "Some people got the publicity they wanted from it. A lot of others tried, and succeeded to a certain extent, to catch on for a free publicity ride. I guess they got what they wanted."

But Ferebee continued to fudge on at least two issues. For nearly 50 years, he insisted that while he had cultivated "a valuable business contact or two" from the marathon, he hadn't pocketed "a dime" from anyone but Tuerk. He would occasionally admit that he had "heard" that by the time he reached Philadelphia the odds against him surviving 600 holes had grown as high as 4–1.

In the year-after interview with Kearns, he even argued that the Internal Revenue Service had already "inquired" about his income for 1938 and had found nothing. That was good enough for Kearns, who published an apology for having questioned Ferebee's motives and integrity.

But in 1986, Ferebee told a close friend, the writer Laurence Leonard of Richmond, Virginia, that he had "run a book" on the marathon, giving odds and taking bets from people who doubted that he could do it. "He found it profitable," Leonard vaguely concluded in his story for the *Senior Golfer* magazine.

The second issue was whether Ferebee really took sole ownership of the 296 acres near Broad Bay Plantation. The answer appears to be no. Records from 1940 show the land still in the names of the wives Jean Tuerk and Angeline Ferebee. The Tuerks may have been paying the mortgage for Ferebee, but it's clear that they never relinquished their rights to the property, which was the supposed crux of the 144-hole wager.

On December 31, 1938, the Ferebees and the Tuerks signed an agreement to lease the land to Frank P. Whitehurst for five years. Any time after the second year, the two families could sell the land but only after giving Whitehurst the opportunity to match any offer. At the top of the contract, the clerk wrote in pencil, "Please do not publish."

Court records in Virginia Beach show that Whitehurst purchased all but approximately 38 acres on July 30, 1943. In May 1954, Jean Tuerk—then divorced from Fred—sold 19 acres to the East Alanton Corporation. Five months later, the Ferebees sold 19 acres to the same corporation, which became part of a Virginia Beach subdivision called Alanton.

Ferebee never realized his dream of living at Broad Bay Manor. He never returned to live in Princess Anne County; instead, he and Angie settled about 90 miles west in Richmond in 1950.

The day after the attack on Pearl Harbor, the 35-year-old Ferebee enlisted in the U.S. Navy. He wanted to fly, but he was nine years older than the age limit. He also lacked a pilot's license, not that he planned to let that detail stop him.

But first, Lieutenant Ferebee was stationed at the Flight Selection Board of Chicago, where his biggest responsibility was selecting a site for a Naval Flight Instructor school. He chose Lockport in Illinois, and when it opened in November 1942, he became its first executive officer.

The position provided him ample opportunity to browbeat his superiors about their decision to keep him behind a desk rather than let him fly. At one point, the navy told him that if he earned a private pilot's license in his spare time they would consider moving him. He did procure one, but they didn't move him.

Then he was told that if he secured a commercial pilot's license, they would consider changing his status. He did that as well, flying more than 100 hours in planes featuring more than 200 horsepower. The navy still ruled that he was too old.

Eventually, Ferebee negotiated a chance to fly. The navy wanted to transfer him to Athens, Georgia. Ferebee agreed to go, but not before arguing that he could do a much better job of recruiting if he was also being trained. He convinced them to let him attend Naval Refresher flight training. Ferebee performed so well there that he was called to active duty in 1942 and a year later—at age 37—he was designated a naval aviator. Thus Ferebee became the oldest officer who had never flown prior to entering the navy to earn his wings.

As usual, Ferebee never backed away from a challenge. In an August 1988 letter of condolence to Angie following Smitty's death, fellow flight instructor Dr. Eugene Beatty wrote about a young cadet teasing Ferebee about his age as Ferebee swam in an Olympic-sized pool at the Glenview Naval Air Station in Illinois.

"So Smitty challenged him to an endurance swim," Beatty noted. "He not only outdistanced this kid but swam twice the number of laps after the boy gave up."

Beatty also recalled Ferebee being obsessed with wanting to experience a parachute jump. Under strict orders not to jump out of any airplanes, one day Ferebee "forgot" to fasten his safety belt as he instructed a cadet to take his plane to 2,000 feet and then roll it over. Ferebee fell out and deployed his chute, though too late to avoid a couple of broken bones when he hit the ground.

"He never stopped amazing me with his capability of achieving most anything he went after," Beatty concluded. "Smitty was a remarkable man, and never stopped amazing me with his physical abilities for he was certainly not the 'macho man' type."

Following his stint at Glenview, Ferebee served aboard the aircraft carrier USS *Belleau Wood*. On August 25, 1945, Ferebee copiloted a plane that crashed while dropping supplies to American prisoners of war north of Tokyo. The pilot died. Ferebee's left arm was broken in 13 places. He also fractured his skull and suffered an internal hemorrhage of his left eye.

Ferebee was ultimately flown to the USS *Benevolence*, where he dictated a letter to a friend and asked him to "let my bride know in the most discreet manner" about his injuries. He confessed that he worried daily that he would lose his eye and that his left arm would have to be amputated.

Ferebee spent nearly a year recuperating from his injuries at the Naval Hospital at Great Lakes, Illinois. He convinced his doctors not to remove his arm. Employing golf as part of his physical therapy, Ferebee recovered partial use of his left arm, though only about 35 percent.

Somehow, that limitation didn't stop him from becoming a major competitor in Virginia State Golf Association senior championships after he and Angie moved to Richmond. In 1962, he won the State Senior Amateur Championship, defeating Marvin Giles, Jr., father of future U.S. and British Amateur champion Marvin "Vinny" Giles III.

As a member of Richmond's Hermitage Country Club, Ferebee continued to play in all kinds of weather and always at breakneck speed. He often walked 18 holes in two hours, or about half the time the U.S. Golf Association mandates for amateur tournaments. He railed against the five-hour rounds that were becoming commonplace in professional golf, and he would have been appalled that today the Professional Golf Association Tour and Ladies Professional Golf Association must resort to levying penalties in order to combat slow play.

In 1939, he promised James Kearns of the *Chicago Daily News* that he was "through with marathons." But in late 1948, Ferebee bet $3,500 that he would shoot 100 rounds of skeet in eight hours and break 70 percent of the birds.

He was better than his word. Averaging one shot every six seconds at Chicago's Lincoln Park Gun Club, Ferebee finished 101 rounds in only four hours and eighteen minutes. He hit 2,121 of 2,525 targets, or 84 percent. *Life* magazine took a photo of him sitting atop a small mountain of spent shells, cradling the fourth shotgun he'd used that day.

After a 20-year career with the Equitable Life Assurance Society in Richmond, Ferebee retired in 1970 and thrust himself into volunteer fund-raising work for the college that expelled him, Virginia Military Institute. He received VMI's Distinguished Service Award in 1981, and although he did not graduate, the institute considers him a member of the class of 1927.

"I am not proud of what I am about to say, yet my teaching at VMI requires me to tell you like it is, so that I do not sail under false colors," he told the student body on the day he received his award. Tearing up, he then recounted the story of his expulsion and of how his mother died "before I could properly demonstrate how much she really meant to me. . . . It will always be my biggest regret that I never graduated from VMI.

"Although I know there are many others who deserve it more than I, I promise to spend the rest of my life being worthy of the honor that I place above all others."

In tribute to Ferebee, the alumni lounge on the third floor of VMI's Clarkson-McKenna Hall-Foster Stadium is named in his honor.

In 1973, Ferebee assembled a coalition of Virginia Republicans, conservative Democrats, and independents in support of incumbent governor Mills Godwin, who won reelection. Later, he served as finance chairman of the state's Republican Party.

In 1983, Ferebee attended a banquet in Richmond. There, the youngest naval pilot to serve in World War II—then vice president George H. W. Bush—asked to be seated next to the oldest naval pilot to serve in that war, Smith Ferebee.

Ferebee died of cancer on July 11, 1988. At his funeral in Richmond, Governor Godwin and Senator Harry F. Byrd, Jr., delivered eulogies.

"Our respect and admiration are always highest, as they should be, for men like Smith Ferebee," Godwin told the congregation, "who could dream great dreams and bring so many of them to reality."

Byrd called Ferebee "unselfish in working for those principles he regarded as being in the best interest of Virginia and our nation."

"I learned very early on that there is one phrase you never used in his presence: 'I cannot,'" said the Reverend Dr. Raymond L. Spence, Ferebee's minister, in his eulogy. "His eyes flashing like coals, his voice rising two octaves, he would repeat, 'You cannot?' then settle you down for all the reasons why you could."

Three days after his death, Ferebee's body was escorted to the family cemetery behind Broad Bay Manor. He had visited there three years before to ask the owner's permission to be buried with the rest of the clan. In a hand-dug grave not far from the land he had "won" from Tuerk 50 years earlier, he was laid to rest under a wild cherry tree.

Angeline Ferebee remained at Logan and Bryan long after Smitty left for Barney Johnson and Company, although she joined him with Equitable at the Warren V. Woody Agency in Chicago. She even occasionally filled in and managed the office when the couple moved to Richmond in 1950.

Reclusive to the end, she died in her home on May 22, 1995, at age 87. She was transported to Virginia Beach and is buried next to her husband in the family cemetery behind Broad Bay Manor.

Fred Tuerk and Ferebee remained close friends until Tuerk's sudden death from a heart attack in 1967. He loved to regale his legion of friends with the story of how he helped make Ferebee temporarily famous, even though a major portion of it came at his expense.

"That never bothered him," said friend and longtime business partner Alex MacWilliam. "I heard about Smitty Ferebee and the golf marathon for years."

Although his wildly fluctuating weight began creating lifelong heart problems for him at an early age, Tuerk was denied military service in World War II because of his partial blindness in one eye. He became president of Chicago-based Utah Radio Products in 1942, overseeing 5,000 employees in the manufacturing of walkie-talkies and headsets for pilots and artillerymen.

In 1944, Tuerk's Chicago plant received the Army-Navy "E" Production Award after tripling its output in one year despite only a 30-percent increase in employees. Many evenings after work, he would head over to the United Service Organization (USO) and cook chop suey for the servicemen.

By 1947, the 42-year-old Tuerk had served five years as governor of the Chicago Stock Exchange. He also was listed on the board of directors of 18 corporations.

Two years later, he moved to Vero Beach, Florida, where he began almost two decades as one of the state's most influential citizens. For someone with such a gargantuan appetite for everything life offered, he started comparatively slowly by purchasing almost 4,000 acres of land that spanned from the ocean to what would become the town of Indian River Shores. Tuerk was mayor there during its first 10 years until he was forced to step down in 1963 for health reasons.

He followed that by acquiring 5,000 more acres and establishing a cattle ranch, even though he didn't know anything about that industry.

"I don't even think he liked cattle ranching, but that was Fred," MacWilliam said. "You never knew what he was going to do from one minute to the next."

However, nothing compared to the next project Tuerk, his cousin Conrad, MacWilliam, and Minute Maid president Holman Cloud undertook. They bought 30,000 acres—all of it under water—then convinced the Florida State legislature to declare it a drainage district and to erect a dike. That process transformed the useless property into a fertile grapefruit and orange grove.

A lifelong Democrat and prominent midwestern fund-raiser, Tuerk and Utah Radio Products partner Dick Norris presented President Harry Truman with a wire recording machine one evening at Blair House, shortly before Truman moved into the White House. In 1945, Truman and New York Stock Exchange president Emil Schram dined at the White House. Afterward, Truman brought Schram and his wife into his office, where he gleefully demonstrated Tuerk and Norris's gift.

"It is sure unique, and he is pleased as punch with it," Schram wrote to Tuerk. "We all made a recording and then listened. . . . The President took great delight in working it."

In addition to politicians, Tuerk loved performers. He was a chief financial backer of *Three to Make Ready*, starring Ray Bolger, which ran on Broadway for 327 performances. Later, he was business partners with Rosalind Russell and her husband Fred Brisson. He was friends with Walter Pidgeon, with the two occasionally lunching at the Pump Room on Chicago's Gold Coast.

In 1963, Tuerk met actress Rhonda Fleming, who suggested to him that he turn one of his islands into a summer and Christmas holiday camp for homeless children. According to gossip columnist Louella Parsons, Tuerk told Fleming that he would give her any of the several islands he owned so that she could pursue the project as she envisioned. Through a representative, Fleming said she remembered the trip and meeting Tuerk, but she could not recall why nothing ever came of the offer.

"Money meant nothing to him," MacWilliam said. "He'd throw a party and he would present every lady in attendance with a ring or a bracelet. He loved going into jewelry stores in New York and Chicago and spending hours negotiating the price of jewelry. And then he'd get home and give it all away."

But other friends jokingly complained that Tuerk never purchased his own hats or hankerchiefs. One year friend John R. Dunbar threw a birthday party for Tuerk at Chicago's Blackstone hotel that made the society pages of a couple of newspapers. Only women were invited, gifts were "obligatory," and the women were asked to bring one of their husband's monogrammed handkerchiefs or one of his older hats.

From 1949 to 1954, he and friend Joseph Nellis funded a scholarship at Denison University in Ohio for rising seniors studying theater arts. The winner would go to New York or Hollywood that summer to study theater or motion picture production techniques.

About his dad, George Tuerk said, "He was the type of man who could walk into a room with fifteen people and dominate it—in a good way. He made friends easily."

During a bash at the Windswept Hotel in Vero Beach, which Tuerk owned, he met a teenage beauty named Adriana Kromhaut. Tuerk separated from his first wife, Jean, in October 1949 and married 18-year-old Adriana in August 1950. The wedding occurred five days after Jean Tuerk won what was, at the time, one of the largest divorce settlements in Reno, Nevada, history: $100,000 cash; $2,000 a month alimony for 12½ years; $5,000 a year each for his children's education; $1,500 a month in child support; a home in Pasadena, California; and an investment account worth approximately $230,000 to which his wife held the title.

Jean insisted that Fred remain part of his children's lives. She refused to give the children their allowance until they had written a weekly letter to their father. The kids spent weeks during the summer with Fred and Adriana.

"He was a wonderful father, not real strict, but very loving," George remembered. "He always was very easy to get along with."

He died of heart failure on February 2, 1967, and was buried in the family cemetery in Indian River Shores.

Reuben Trane continued as the president of the Trane Company until 1951 when he became chairman of the Board of Directors. He earned 27 patents in the fields of air-conditioning and heating and was inducted into the American Society of Heating Refrigeration and Air-Conditioning Engineers Hall of Fame in 1997.

During World War II, he developed and manufactured an intercooler for high-altitude airplanes that was one-third the weight, occupied one-fourth of the space, and was half as expensive as the previous model. His company also developed and produced deicing equipment for airplane wings, cooled plane cabins, turned seawater into distilled water for drinking, and ventilated ships and war plants.

Much less known was his company's contribution to the Manhattan Project. According to a 2005 story in the *La Crosse Tribune*, project officials approached Trane at his headquarters in January 1945, because Trane manufactured drawn aluminum tubes. They told him that they needed the tooling to produce special aluminum tubes, and that the request should be treated as the highest priority. They never mentioned an atomic bomb.

Trane introduced them to Einar Lunde, who at the time ran the tool and die department. When Lunde assured these officials that he could produce what they needed, Trane gave his permission for Lunde to begin work in Chicago immediately. Only after he was sworn to secrecy was he told the nature of his new assignment.

When the war ended, Reuben Trane turned to developing the refrigeration of railroad freight cars to safely transport frozen foods across the country. He then employed the same principles to become a pioneer in the air-conditioning of cars and buses.

After a lengthy illness, Trane died on September 5, 1954, at age 67 and is buried in La Crosse, Wisconsin. At the time of his death, Trane Company sales had risen from $50,000 in 1913 to more than $50 million.

Dr. Charles Alexander continued practicing medicine in Harvey, Illinois, serving as the chairman of the surgical staff at Ingalls Memorial Hospital and as the medical director for the Whiting Corporation. His passion for helping underprivileged youth led him to become a member of the Board of Trustees for what was then known as the Glenwood School for Boys.

Dr. Alexander maintained his membership at Olympia Fields until 1959, when he moved to Palm Desert, California. There, he served on the staff of Desert Hospital. He died on April 10, 1966, at age 71, and is buried in his birthplace of Cooperstown, Pennsylvania.

Capt. Edward C. Bowe remained with American Airlines until his retirement in December 1959. During World War II, he flew 106 Atlantic crossings, carrying army troops overseas as part of American Airlnes' contract with the Air Transport Command.

Bowe flew out of Los Angeles from 1945 to 1955 and then moved to Fort Worth, Texas, until his retirement. He was one of the founding members of the Grey Eagles, an organization for American Airlines pilots 50 years of age and older.

Captain Bowe "flew west" after suffering a massive coronary on July 10, 1973, at age 67. He is buried in McAllen, Texas.

Lillian Fette remained with American Airlines until 1939. Some of her more famous passengers were Eleanor Roosevelt, Clark Gable, and the Four Horsemen of Notre Dame football lore. After leaving the airline, she modeled and continued doing commercials for Pepsodent.

She married Thomas Gallery, one-time director of NBC Sports. She died on August 7, 1997, at the age of 85.

Adolph Oettinger Goodwin lived only another five years following the completion of the marathon. He moved from Chicago to Detroit, where he took a position with an advertising firm until his retirement in 1941. In March 1943, Goodwin moved into the Veterans Hospital in Memphis, Tennessee, where he died on June 9.

Art Caschetta, the boy caddie, was the only member of Ferebee's marathon party still alive at the time this book was written.

He served in the U.S. Navy from 1940 to 1946, including an assignment aboard the USS *Carlisle*. After the war, he returned to Olympia Fields, where he became caddie master from 1960 until 1972. Overall, he spent 62 years there, working in the locker room, shoe room, engine room, carpenter shop, and carts department. Caschetta helped build the dance floor at Olympia Fields and was Santa Claus at the club's Christmas party. He even ran the skeet-shooting operation in the winter.

"That club gave me an education beyond my dreams," he told the club's in-house *Olympian* magazine in 2007. "I wouldn't trade it for the world."

Working by his side all those years was his wife, Mary. He had brought her family hot dogs the day he helped Ferebee beat Riffle with the $1,000 putt. Mary and Art retired to Florida together in 1999; on June 9, 2010, Mary passed away. Art remains in Florida.

Finally, what of the eight country clubs that served as Ferebee's canvas? Do they still exist? Could someone walk in Ferebee's footsteps and replicate the 600-hole marathon?

The answer to the last question, sadly, is no.

Lakeside, the golfing home to Hope, Crosby, W. C. Fields, Humphrey Bogart, John Wayne, and, of course, Gene Autry, remains private and aloof. A 2008 story in the *Burbank Leader* stated that the club "gave area golf enthusiasts a rare and excusive opportunity to see" its grounds when it allowed spectators to watch the 97th annual California Amateur Championship.

Encanto in Phoenix, meanwhile, markets itself as "ideally suited for the average golfer." It touts its open fairways and limited number of hazards. The course opens 30 minutes before dawn each day, including holidays, year-round. The third-oldest course in Arizona, it offers spectacular views of downtown Phoenix.

Blue Hills Country Club in Kansas City was moved from the site where Ferebee played to a different location in 1962 in conjunction with the club's 50th anniversary. Club officials swapped their 117 acres, including the course and facilities, for 155 acres at a location south of 125th Street off State Line. The swap was proposed and orchestrated by a local developer named Bill Bushman, who agreed to fund the construction of the new clubhouse and golf course as part of the deal. He built a shopping center on the original site.

For 25 years, Blue Hills and golf legend Tom Watson, winner of eight "major" championships and 39 total events, worked together to host the Children's Mercy Hospital Golf Classic. Watson, an honorary member of Blue Hills, hosted four of the game's greatest names—Jack Nicklaus, Arnold Palmer, Gary Player, and Lee Trevino—and raised more than $10 million.

Norwood Hills in St. Louis remains a private club with two 18-hole championship golf courses. In 2005, it was placed on the National Register of Historical Places, as determined by the U.S. Department of the Interior.

Like Blue Hills, Milwaukee's Tuckaway still exists and remains closed to the public. But it is not at the location Ferebee visited, the club having moved to Franklin, Wisconsin, in 1968. The old site, though short, offered enough shot-making challenges that the Ladies Professional Golf Association played the Milwaukee Open there in 1962 and 1966.

In 1968, however, the club moved south to a 285-acre site that included a 33,000-square foot, bi-level clubhouse. The new Tuckaway gained some notoriety from 1973 through 1993 when the PGA Tour played the Greater Milwaukee Open there. Jack Nicklaus, Lee Trevino, and the late Payne Stewart extolled the virtues of the 7,000-yard-plus layout. Tuckaway relinquished the event in 1994.

Olympia Fields, Ferebee's home course, remains private but has changed dramatically since he was a member. It ran into financial difficulties during World War II and was forced to sell half of its land. The result was the loss of two of the club's four courses, though several holes were integrated from the East and West Courses (Numbers 2 and 3) to help form the South Course.

The North Course remains ranked among the top 50 in the United States and was host to the 1928 and 2003 U.S. Open and the 1925 and 1961 PGA Championships. Walter Hagen and Johnny Farrell won the '25 PGA and '28 U.S. Open, respectively, while Jerry Barber won the '61 PGA and Jim Furyk captured the '03 U.S. Open.

In 2001, Olympia Fields was added to the National Register of Historic Places.

North Hills Country Club outside Philadelphia remains private and vibrant. However, the club lost an iconic leader in 2010 when 67-year-old Ron Rolfe, its pro for more than 40 years, died suddenly of a heart attack. A member of the Philadelphia Section PGA Hall of Fame, Ron was well known throughout Philadelphia for helping suburban high school golf teams secure courses on which to practice and play.

The story of Salisbury Country Club, where Ferebee ended the marathon, is bittersweet. Once a megacomplex with five courses, Salisbury's ownership could not meet the tax burden during the Depression. Nassau County took over the property, added land, and opened all of its amenities to the public.

In 1944 Salisbury Country Club became Nassau County Park at Salisbury. Twenty-five years later, it was rededicated as Dwight D. Eisenhower Memorial Park.

Today, there are three courses, designated Red, White, and Blue. Ferebee played the Red Course, which later was lengthened and from 1998 to 2008 hosted the Commerce Bank Championship on the PGA's Champions Tour. Loren Roberts won the final tournament staged there and the $240,000 first prize.

At 930 acres, Eisenhower Park is larger than Central Park. It offers a pool and fitness center at the world-class Nassau County Aquatic Center; a batting cage; athletic fields; playgrounds; a two-mile fitness trail; basketball and tennis courts; boccie and lawn bowling; and the Harry Chapin Lakeside Theatre.

It also features a memorial to the victims of the terrorist attack on September 11, 2001, that includes steel from the World Trade Center. President George W. Bush attended the memorial's groundbreaking ceremony in 2004.

Author's Notes

Conspicuous by its absence in chapter 11 is the fate of Fidelus A. Notty, also known as The Tall Man. Unlike all of the other characters—Ferebee, Tuerk, Alexander, Bowe, Fette, Goodwin, Pederson, Caschetta, and even Snowball, the dog—The Tall Man emerged from my imagination, as did the men of the ten syndicates. However, I did not create The Tall Man on a whim or out of whole cloth; quite the contrary.

Over the course of five years, I made every effort to identify and locate anyone who witnessed or was part of Ferebee's 600-hole golf marathon of 1938. The only truly knowledgeable person I found was Art Caschetta. However, thanks to golf professional Ron Rolfe, on the second of three trips to North Hills Country Club outside Philadelphia, I conducted an interview with Lawrence "Pratt" Coleman. He was a child, not even in school yet, on the morning Ferebee arrived at the club. A kid who shagged golf balls on the practice range, he did not follow Ferebee until after his first round. The breakfast buffet outside the clubhouse at North Hills, he admitted with glee almost seventy years later, was available to anyone and loaded with enough goodies to make watching golf in the dark and fog completely unappealing.

Coleman remembered an acquaintance of his, now long deceased, venturing onto the course to watch a few of Ferebee's early holes. He returned and told Coleman that he couldn't understand how Ferebee had progressed as far as he had in the marathon, for he was playing golf that early morning "like he was drunk." Or drugged?

Other factors were considered. There was Caschetta's suspicion that something crooked was afoot during the first round. Yes, Ferebee's game could be spectacularly erratic, though that makes the fact that his second-, third-, and fourth-round scores were 14, 14, and 12 strokes lower than his opening 18 even more suspicious.

Furthermore, in the script he coauthored for the October 11, 1938, broadcast of *We the People*, Ferebee confessed that, "Believe me man, I still don't remember those first 18 holes [at Philadelphia]. . . . I played that round in my sleep."

Considering the amount of money at stake, Ferebee's clandestine bookmaking operation, and North Hills' reputation as a haven for gamblers, creating a character to embody those elements seemed not only logical but also fundamental.

The Sharp Stick is loosely based on Philadelphia's famous Cherry Street Tavern, which has been in business in the same location since the early 1900s. (During Prohibition, it was a barber shop that reportedly offered men pleasures beyond those derived from a precision haircut. There was a side entrance women used that took them to a back room.)

Another issue I grappled with was whether to accept the Ferebee publicity team's claim that the *TRANE of the Air* Douglas DC-3 was the first air-conditioned plane in aviation history. From my initial perspective, it made little sense for the team to fabricate such a story; yet in the hundreds of newspaper clippings I found, it never received more than a cursory mention, at best. Why?

Fortunately, I encountered four men whose combined knowledge allowed me to conclude that the claim made in this regard was pure hyperbole. Under their guidance, I decided to err on the side of caution and omit it from the story.

Start with Jeffrey Johns, curator of the C. R. Smith American Airlines Museum in Dallas, Texas. Mr. Johns's uncommon diligence in helping locate the maintenance log for the DC-3, plus information on Capt. Ed Bowe and photos of the plane itself, was an enormous, welcome surprise. Henry M. Holden, author and aviation historian, was most gracious in a series of e-mails that answered my rather elementary questions about the Douglas DC-3. He also analyzed the maintenance log that Mr. Johns found and assured me that the record showed no extraordinary work had been done to the plane.

Bernard Nagengast, author and air-conditioning historian, supplied a magazine story from 1936—two years before Ferebee's marathon—on methods airlines were beginning to implement to air-condition their planes.

Finally, Art Scheskie at Trane headquarters searched the company's archives for any record of the company being the first to air-condition an airplane. He could find nothing other than an in-house magazine story that mentioned the "fact" almost in passing. It seemed a funny way for any company to treat a supposed history-making accomplishment and made it easier to believe that the story wasn't true.

The other missing link is the stowaway, Al Knoebel, if that is indeed how he spelled his name. It seemed to be spelled differently in every newspaper story in which he was mentioned. Al really existed and really was on the airplane, as shown in a couple of the photos included herein. Caschetta said more than once that while he wasn't sure, he suspected that Al was part of the plan from the beginning, a pawn injected into the story for some additional drama. Art never saw the young man again. I made every effort to find Al or some relative or descendant, without success.

Perhaps the most amazing aspect of the story behind the story is that even when relatives of the principle characters were found, the vast majority of them had no idea that their fathers had ever participated in such a wild stunt. Some, such as Reuben Trane's son, Frank, found it almost impossible to believe that his father would be involved in something so impetuous and costly. Some of them were grateful to learn something new and unexpected about their fathers.

Along the way, some minor family mysteries were solved. George Tuerk, Fred's son and a wonderful, engaging confidant, owned a photo of his father sitting atop an elephant. George had no clue as to how he got there or why. After months of daily newspaper research, I finally uncovered the story.

Shortly after Ferebee's 144-hole marathon in August 1938, a broker named Johnny "Ha Ha" Heronymus invited fellow professionals from Milwaukee, Chicago, and St. Louis to play golf at Pine Hills Country Club in Sheboygan, Wisconsin. Ferebee, accompanied by Tuerk, was the guest of honor and accorded the "privilege" of riding around the golf course aboard an elephant Heronymus had rented for the occasion. As George's photo shows, Tuerk spent some time in the saddle, too.

As an aside, one of George Tuerk's goals is to buy a racehorse and name him Smitty Ferebee.

Madelyn Alexander, Dr. Charles Alexander's always gracious, giving daughter, solved the mystery of how Gene Autry became involved with the Ferebee party by sharing her insight into the relationship her father had with the Hollywood star.

Alex MacWilliam, a close friend and business partner of Fred Tuerk's, helped me understand the man better during a long and candid phone conversation.

Fred Pederson's widow, Adeline, and daughter Ellen Horak were kind enough to sift through some old photos and provide a couple of Fred following the marathon.

It should be obvious by now that no one writes a book such as this one alone. I can't imagine another writer receiving as much assistance as I was blessed to have come my way. I list the following names in no particular order and with near-equal degrees of appreciation. Each played a key role in whatever success *King of Clubs* achieves; conversely, I am solely responsible for any of its shortcomings.

Family members who did what they could to help include cousin John T. Ferebee, now deceased. Betsy Duerr, Fred Tuerk's daughter, buoyed my spirits with her enthusiasm and immediate interest. I thank Don Alexander, the grandson of Dr. Charles Alexander, and Bruce Bowe, son of DC-3 pilot Ed Bowe.

I am deeply grateful to agent Jake Elwell of Harold Ober Associates in New York for his unending enthusiasm for this project. I am astounded at the passion and caring with which he answered a cold-call e-mail and the tenacity with which he pursued a home for Smitty's story.

Likewise, my gratitude goes to former sports columnist Thom Loverro of the *Washington Times*, who recommended Jake during a conversation in the press box at FedEx Field prior to a Washington Redskins home game. Actually, Thom did more than just recommend Jake; the next morning he made good on his promise to contact Jake and ask if he had any interest in the story of a crazy golf bet from the late 1930s.

The crew at Potomac Books, Inc., especially editor Elizabeth Demers, the brilliantly thorough and inquisitive Vicki Chamlee, Kathryn Owens, Elizabeth Norris, Sam Dorrance, Maryam Rostamian, and Laura Briggs, deserves the highest praise for guiding the story through to its conclusion. I hope *King of Clubs* will be the first of many joint ventures.

Special thanks as well go to Giff Breed of Octagon, the extraordinary sports and entertainment marketing agency.

Then there's Art Caschetta, the only living member of the Ferebee entourage. I'll never forget the look on Art's face as we sat in his kitchen in Florida and he recounted his version of the Ferebee story. He and his vivacious wife, Mary, were enduring a family health crisis at the time, and the hospitality and enthusiasm with which they greeted my wife and me will never be forgotten.

Among Ferebee's friends, special thanks go to Eddie Swink, Elmon Gray, and Bowlman Bowles, who helped shed some much-needed light on Angie. Chet Ehrenzeller, owner of Broad Bay Manor, didn't have a close relationship with Ferebee, but he opened his home, Smitty's birthplace, to him on several occasions. When Ferebee died in 1988, Ehrenzeller dug his grave by hand. Seven years later, he repeated the process for Angie.

King of Clubs started with a simple Internet search that turned up information that Angie Ferebee had bequeathed marathon-related information to Virginia Military Institute. That link took me to Diane Jacob, head of archives and record management, and her assistant, Mary Laura Kludy. They couldn't have been more helpful, informative, and diligent in filling a variety of requests.

As always, the staff at the Library of Congress transformed what could have been long, fruitless days into productive and pleasurable excursions that I will miss until I undertake my next project. Likewise, the staff of the Williamsburg, Virginia, Public Library offered invaluable assistance on countless occasions

Anita Doering of the La Crosse, Wisconsin, Public Library, a delightful personality, produced vital information on Reuben Trane. And Anna FitzSimmons of the Illinois Newspaper Project unearthed several invaluable stories for me, after I'd given up hope of finding anything new on Ferebee from Illinois-area publications. Ann Johnson and Maureen Watts from the library staff at the *Virginian-Pilot* tracked down an obituary of Adolph O. Goodwin, virtually the only information on him that an exhaustive search turned up. Librarian Donna Colletta at the *Arizona Republic* found some history on the Encanto Golf Course.

Although Ferebee saved a written transcript of his 1938 interview with Robert Ripley, which is quoted and paraphrased in chapter 4, Edward Meyer of Ripley Entertainment, Inc., was quick to respond to questions regarding radio programs of the late 1930s. Historian Stephen Mansfield of Virginia Wesleyan College in Virginia Beach walked me through a vintage map or two of the area around Broad Bay one afternoon.

Two of the clubs where Ferebee played—Blue Hills in Kansas City and Tuckaway in Milwaukee—have moved from their locations in 1938. Sadly, with those moves comes the inevitable disposal of potentially valuable historical documentation. Neither club was able to assist with any aspect of the Ferebee story, but I thank Milwaukee researcher Jean Straub for fleshing out life at Tuckaway in the 1930s. In addition, Victoria Aspinwall of Hofstra University assisted with information on the Salisbury Country Club.

I personally visited Encanto Golf Club in Phoenix, Norwood Hills in St. Louis, Olympia Fields in Chicago, and North Hills in Philadelphia. Gwen Russell of Olympia Fields, a membership director imbued with a historian's soul, couldn't have been more accommodating. She met me at the train station at the club's back gate, hauled me anywhere she thought might be of some interest, and provided me with copies of decades' worth of the club's board meeting minutes that helped bring alive many aspects of the club's life.

At Norwood Hills, John Wright helped make my visit one of the early joys of the research process. The man had snow, ice, and a club Christmas party to worry about, but he not only managed to spend a couple of hours personally with me but also followed up with several encouraging e-mails. At North Hills Country Club outside Philadelphia, the late golf pro Ron Rolfe and member Jack Darcy were so kind with their time and tales that they made me wish I lived much, much closer to their fabulous club. Gene Contino of Nassau County Parks and Recreation was a huge help with information and a map of Salisbury Country Club, now Dwight D. Eisenhower Memorial Park's Red Course, on Long Island.

At the top of the list of my friends and supporters is PGA golf professional Butch Liebler, who critiqued my early work and helped with some of the technical aspects of golf. In addition, we engaged in dozens of encouraging conversations that reinforced the importance of this project to me.

I thank sportswriters John Keim, Rick Snider, Dave Elfin, Ryan O'Halloran, Dan Daly, and Paul Woody for their support and friendship. Daly also guided me through some early Internet research. Likewise, author extraordinaire Earl Swift, my former colleague at the *Virginian-Pilot*, has my gratitude for his support and guidance through the early stages of this project. While in New York on business, my friend John Kollmansperger visited the public library and conducted some research on communication between Ferebee party members and the 1939 World's Fair Committee.

I am grateful to Jamie Conkling, executive director of the Virginia State Golf Association, for putting me in touch with Bob Thomas and Kevin Heaney of the Southern California Golf Association, who assisted my search for information on Lakeside Country Club. Also, thanks to writer Mike DiGiovanna of the *Los Angeles Times.*

Everyone needs an audience in order to judge whether he's headed in the right direction. I was lucky beyond belief to have group leaders Rick and Emeline Bailey and the rest of the Williamsburg Critique Group listen and provide feedback. In addition, Doug and Sebastiana Springmann offered encouragement and advice that opened new doors for me.

I never would have made it this far without the help and guidance of editor Sofia Starnes of Williamsburg. Her attention to detail, thorough but fair criticism, and helpful suggestions served to improve this work beyond what I ever could have done on my own.

To the wonderful friends and professionals at the College of William & Mary—Brian, Suzanne, Erin, Stephen, David, Joe, Gabi, Megan, Cindi, and Teri—thank you all. To Justin Schoonmaker of the college's Creative Services Department, I greatly appreciate your help and guidance with the photos contained herein.

Last, and obviously not least, I thank my family for everything they've had to deal with the past five-plus years. My dad, Jim, was never anything less than encouraging, even when the process seemed to drag on beyond reason. My daughter Stephanie was on board with the project from the start. She was generous with her enthusiasm, encouragement, and interest, all of which helped lift my spirits. My daughter Katherine offered the same and aided me in an exhausting—and hopefully exhaustive—investigation of Virginia Beach real estate records.

Finally, there's my long-suffering wife, Sue, who traveled with me, listened attentively to my gripes and fears, and watched in silence as I spent money we didn't have for research. Sue helped in every way she could, reading all my work with a critical eye when I asked her, and over five years never said anything more discouraging than "just do your best."

Hers was the best advice anyone offered. I can honestly say I tried to follow it with every keystroke.

Source Notes

1. Some Real Money

The opening locker-room scene and the decision to play the 144 holes when Angie Ferebee was out of town were taken from Ferebee's description of events as reported by the Associated Press, the script for the October 11, 1938, radio program *We the People* that Ferebee cowrote with David Eisenberg, and a document entitled "The History of J. Smith Ferebee" from his file with Barney Johnson and Company that was distributed to media during the 600-hole marathon.

Quotes from Art Caschetta were taken from my interviews with him. He also told me the story of Ferebee sinking a putt to win $1,000 from Adam Riffel.

The anecdote of Ferebee tossing nickels to kids at Olympia Fields and telling them to buy ice cream was taken from my interview with Ferebee's friend Eddie Swink.

2. A Ferebee Never Quits

Ferebee said, "I like to accomplish things. . . ," to Eddie Swink and many others throughout his life. U.S. senator Harry F. Byrd Jr., quoted him in the eulogy he delivered at Ferebee's funeral. Angie Ferebee saved a copy and eventually bequeathed it to Virginia Military Institute.

Information on Ferebee swimming from Virginia Beach to Cape Henry Lighthouse was provided to the *Norfolk Virginian-Pilot* in 1938 by a relative who, according to the newspaper, "asked that his name not be used."

The dialogue between Ferebee and his father was adapted primarily from Ferebee's description of their relationship to his friend Eddie Swink.

Correspondence between Ferebee's mother, Eva Ferebee, and Virginia Military Institute superintendent W. H. Cocke was excerpted from letters exchanged between the two that Eva had saved.

"Mine was the act of a fool . . . " and all subsequent quotes regarding reinstatement to Virginia Military Institute were taken from letters that Ferebee wrote to Cocke, copies of which Ferebee had saved. Angie Ferebee found them in papers bequeathed to Virginia Military Institute after her husband's death.

"In talking to him . . . " was taken from W. J. Dixon's letter to Cocke, a copy of which Ferebee saved.

Ferebee's meeting with Walter Darfler and the dialogue between them was taken primarily from Ferebee's account to the *Richmond News Leader*.

The ten black-eyed peas story was one that Ferebee's friend Eddie Swink related to me. Ferebee told it to him during their many drives together from Richmond to VMI to attend sporting and alumni events during the 1970s and '80s.

3. Quantity over Quality

The scene waiting for Ferebee when he arrived at Olympia Fields was taken from my interviews with Art Caschetta.

Ferebee's dinner selection the night before he played the 144 holes was included in a report in the *Chicago Evening American*.

The details of how the media covered Ferebee's 144-hole marathon, including the need for additional switchboard operators at the *Tribune*, was taken from *Editor & Publisher* magazine.

The radio announcer's gaffe at believing that Ferebee deliberately hit a shot off a rock in Butterfield Creek and onto the green was found in a retrospective piece in *Senior Golfer* magazine. A slightly different version—the ball landed in the fairway, not the green—was included in a shot-by-shot sidebar in what was then the *Chicago Daily Tribune*.

Some of the details of Ferebee's play, such as his putting out of sand traps, were provided in my interviews with Art Caschetta.

4. Believe It or Not

Earl Hilligan's Associated Press account of Ferebee's 144-hole event appeared in innumerable newspapers across the country. "Did everything he said he would . . . " was found in many papers.

Charles Bartlett's description of the event as "one of the most amazing marathons for a strange stake the game has ever seen" was taken from one of his stories in the *Chicago Daily Tribune*.

Ripley's quote from Ferebee's appearance on his program was taken from a written transcript of the show found in papers Angie Ferebee bequeathed to VMI following her husband's death.

Information on the various marathons played following Ferebee's appearance on *Ripley's Believe It or Not* was gained from research using www.news paperarchive.com for the period between the 144-hole event in August 1938 and the announcement of the 600-hole marathon in September. Those papers included the *Lowell (MA) Sun, Joplin (MO) Globe, Edwardsville (IL) Intelligencer, San Antonio Light, Gettysburg (PA) Times, Titusville (PA) Herald, Wisconsin State Journal, Capital (WI) Times, Oshkosh (WI) Northwestern, Oelwein (IA) Daily Register, Middletown (NY) Times Herald, Newark (OH) Advocate, Olean (NY) Times-Herald, El Paso Herald-Post*, and *Vidette-Messenger* of Valparaiso, Indiana.

5. A Trane Arrives

Some details of Fred Tuerk's second challenge to Ferebee were taken from the October 11, 1938, script for *We the People* that Ferebee cowrote with David Eisenberg, as well as from the "History of J. Smith Ferebee" document in his file with Barney Johnson and Company.

Information on Reuben Trane and improvements to air-conditioning was compiled from many sources, most essentially the *La Crosse (WI) Tribune*. Also the La Crosse Public Library archives; James M. Ritter, chapter historian, La Crosse Area Chapter of the American Society of Heating, Refrigerating, and Air-Conditioning Engineers, "The History of a Person: Reuben N. Trane," an entry in the "Gold Ribbon and Log Book of TIME" series, 1993; *Time* magazine; the American Society of Heating, Refrigerating, and Air-Conditioning Engineers; the website for Trane, Inc., http://

www.trane.com; the Wisconsin Historical Society; the Trane Company; the National Academy of Engineering, "10. Air Conditioning and Refrigeration," *Greatest Engineering Achievements of the 20th Century*, 2011, www.greatachievements.org; Ibis Communications, "Air-Conditioning Goes to the Movies, 1925," EyeWitness to History, 2007, www.eye witness tohistory.com/ac.htm; and correspondence with engineer and air-conditioning expert Bernard Nagengast.

Examples of Trane's marketing methods were taken from advertisements from mid-1930s editions of the *Wisconsin State Journal, Oshkosh (WI) Northwestern,* and *Capital (WI) Times.*

Information on the background check that World's Fair officials conducted on Ferebee was taken from actual copies of telegrams between *Chicago Evening American* columnist Ed Cochrane, *Evening American* reporter Bill Margolis, and World's Fair official Jack Reilly. They were found at the New York City Public Library.

Details of Libbie Maxwell's suit against "Big Bill" Johnson came from a September 5, 1938, *Time* magazine story.

6. Shooting Stars

Alexander's daughter Madelyn furnished the details of Dr. Charles Alexander's relationship with Gene Autry. That Autry was a member of Lakeside Country Club in Burbank was confirmed from various accounts of his life.

We know that Ferebee stayed in room 4333 at the Biltmore because he saved a phone message note with his name and the room number on it.

The details of Ferebee and Trane's after-golf exploits in Hollywood were furnished by an interview with Ferebee's friend Eddie Swink, a *Chicago Evening American* column by Ed Cochrane, and a Trane Company commemorative publication, "The Marathon to End All Golf Marathons," which was distributed to sales staff and customers in November 1938. A copy was provided to me courtesy of Trane and was found in Ferebee's papers at Virginia Military Institute.

Information regarding the DC-3 Skysleeper was gathered from my visit to the C. R. Smith American Airlines Museum in Dallas, where one is on display; Henry Holden's *The Legacy of the DC-3* (Stockton, CA: Wind Canyon Publishing, 1996); and the Trane commemorative publication "The Marathon to End All Golf Marathons" from November 1938.

The story of T. Redmond Flood's gift of Cur-A-Ped cream to Ferebee was taken from the letter, which Ferebee saved, that Flood wrote to Ferebee seeking an introduction.

The actors and actresses listed as watching Ferebee at Lakeside were taken from Ferebee's recollections to newspapers and friends. Friends of Ferebee's recall that because of the marathon, he also developed lifelong friendships with actors Joseph Cotten and Richard Arlen.

7. A Snowball's Chance

Some of the biographical information on Capt. Ed Bowe was taken from the application form he filled out when joining the Grey Eagles, the American Airlines pilots' alumni association.

Some of stewardess Lillian Fette's background information was taken from Gwen Mahler's *Wings of Excellence: American Airlines Flight Attendants, a Pictorial History, 1933–1993* (Marceline, MO: Walsworth, 1993), and provided by the C. R. Smith American Airlines Museum. Other information was gathered from the *La Crosse Tribune*, her Aquinas High School yearbook, and her daughters.

The description of the conditions aboard the DC-3 that prevented Ferebee from sleeping was taken from several sources, including the script for the October 11, 1938, broadcast of *We the People* that Ferebee cowrote with David Eisenberg. Details of Ferebee's trip from the Kansas City airport to Blue Hills were taken from the *Kansas City Times*.

Details of the individual stops on the 600-hole marathon were taken from wire-service reports, the local newspapers in each city, and the Trane commemorative publication "The Marathon to End All Golf Marathons," November 1938. Some papers carried the names of the individuals who won the $100 bills from Trane. I included them when available. The story of Snowball the dog was compiled from my interviews with Art Caschetta, George Tuerk, and Eddie Swink and from photos and text in Kansas City papers. The history of Norwood Hills Country Club in St. Louis was compiled during my visit and tour of the club and from the book *Norwood Hills Country Club: A Family Tradition* (no author or publisher credited).

8. Midwest Madness

Stories about Tuckaway Country Club members were taken from the club's 1928 annual report.

The Ferebee–Burle Gose look-alike anecdote was taken from the *Milwaukee News*.

The exchange between Ferebee and the stowaway was re-created from Ferebee's recollection of events as told to several newspapers, as well as my interview with Art Caschetta.

Olympia Fields' welcome for Ferebee was taken from my search through the minutes of monthly club meetings and newspaper accounts by Bill Margolis of the *Chicago Evening American*.

9. A Dangerous Fog in Philadelphia

Details of North Hills Country Club's history were provided by the club and found in the *Philadelphia Evening Bulletin* and *Philadelphia Public Ledger*.

When discussing his physical and mental state during his opening round at North Hills, Ferebee wrote in the script for the October 11, 1938, broadcast of *We the People* that "I don't even remember those first 18 holes."

10. A Ghostly Trail

Jack Reilly's memo to the World's Fair committee regarding Ferebee's arrival was taken exclusively from a copy of the memo found at the New York City public library.

The lengths to which Dr. Charles Alexander went to treat Ferebee's blisters was covered in several newspapers and in retrospective treatments of the marathon, including the *Milwaukee News*, the *St. Louis Daily Globe-Democrat*, the *Los Angeles Examiner*, the Trane commemorative publication "The Marathon to End All Golf Marathons," and the *Philadelphia Inquirer*.

Salisbury pro Pete Cassella's taking over the final portion of the marathon was covered in the script Ferebee cowrote for the October 11, 1938, broadcast of *We the People*.

The "Don't disturb 'til XMAS" anecdote was taken from several accounts of the marathon, including *Time* magazine's.

11. Closing the Books

That Ferebee did not lose a ball in 600 holes remains one of the most amazing sidelights to the marathon. Some people believe he played with the same ball all four days. Not true. Art Caschetta said that while they did not lose a ball, they changed golf balls when necessary.

Information on Ferebee's increased dedication to improving his golf was provided by my interviews with Art Caschetta.

At one point in the months following the marathon, Ferebee appeared bitter at having been talked into participating in the publicity campaign for Trane products. That conclusion was drawn from his exchange of letters with Trane and his one-year-later interview with James Kearns of the *Chicago Daily News.*

Information about the 1940 Whitehurst lease and subsequent sale of the property came from the City of Virginia Beach.

Dr. Beatty's letter to Angie was provided to me during my interview with Ferebee's family attorney Bowlman Bowles of Richmond, Virginia.

Ferebee's loss to Adam Riffel in the Olympia Fields Club Championship was taken from minutes of the club's monthly meetings.

Ferebee's story of breaking par at Olympia Fields' Course Number 4 on December 7, 1941, came from a story in the *Richmond News Leader.*

Information on Ferebee's early attempts to fly in the war, and not be a flight instructor, was taken from my interview with Ferebee's friend Eddie Swink; a profile of Ferebee in *Upcheck* magazine, July 1943; the *Richmond News Leader;* and *Style* magazine.

The quotes from Ferebee's eulogies were taken from copies found in the papers bequeathed to VMI.

The anecdote of Fred Tuerk cooking chop suey for servicemen at the Chicago USO came from his son, George Tuerk.

New York Stock Exchange (NYSE) president Emil Schram's note to Fred Tuerk on Harry Truman's reaction to the "recording machine" Tuerk and partner Dick Norris presented to the president was provided by Tuerk's daughter, Betsy Duerr, as were all media accounts of his real estate deals.

The terms of Tuerk's divorce settlement were taken from the *Chicago Herald-American,* the *Chicago Sun-Times,* and my interview with Tuerk's friend and occasional business partner Alex MacWilliam.

About the Author

The first thing Jim Ducibella dreamed of being—other than a professional golfer who won tournaments, the hearts of fans, and millions of dollars without ever spending a moment on the practice range—was a professional writer. The last thing he ever dreamed of was being inducted into *anyone's* hall of fame. Somehow, both occurred.

Ducibella has been writing professionally, or at least getting paid for it, since a too-brief stint at the late, lamented *Washington Star* from 1979 to 1981. From 1981 to 2008, he was the lead writer covering pro football and golf at the *Virginian-Pilot* in Norfolk, where his peers voted him the state's sportswriter of the year seven times.

In 2010, he was inducted into the Virginia Sports Hall of Fame. He is part of a class that included former basketball superstar Alonzo Mourning and former pro football stars Herman Moore and Jim Dombrowski.

The author of the 2000 book *Par Excellence: A Celebration of Virginia Golf* (Sports Publishing), Ducibella now writes for the College of William & Mary's University Relations bureau. He also contributes a back-page column for *Virginia Golfer* magazine and is a frequent contributor to *Boomer* magazine.

Ducibella and his wife, Sue, have two terrific adult daughters, Stephanie in Chantilly, Virginia, and Katherine in Norfolk, Virginia. The men in their lives, Chris and Eric, are pretty terrific, too. Sue and Jim live with Tucker, the wonder dog, in Williamsburg, Virginia.